TUTORING: ONE TO ONE
READING, WRITING AND RELATING

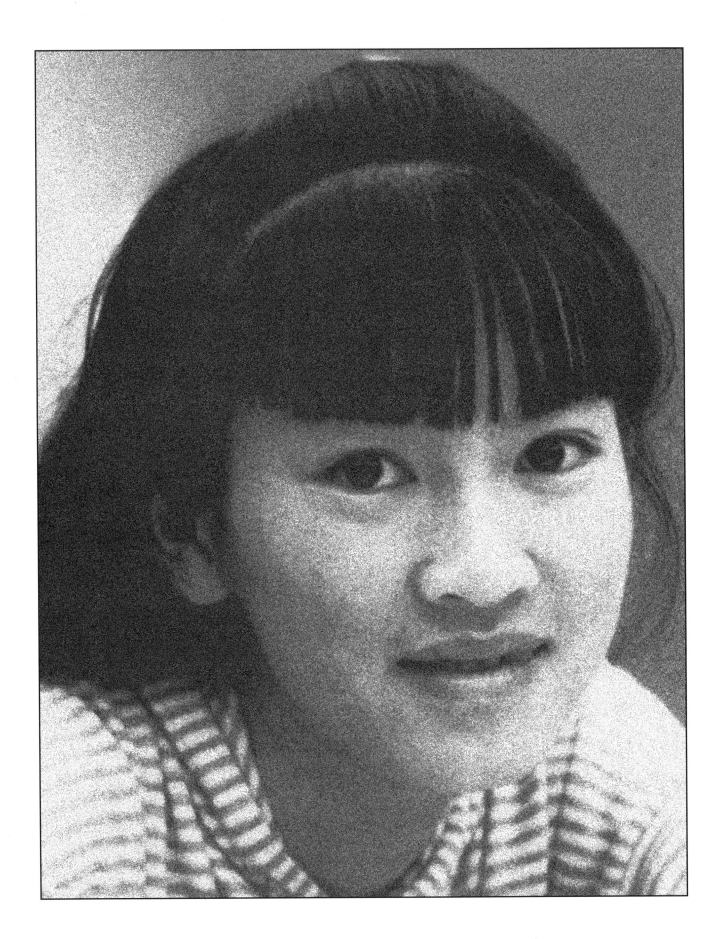

DONALD M. JONES

TUTORING: ONE TO ONE
READING, WRITING AND RELATING

PAEDAGOGUS PUBLISHING INC.

Published in 1994 by:

Paedagogus Publishing Inc.
P.O. Box 604
Peterborough, Ontario
K9J 6Z8

CANADIAN CATALOGUING IN PUBLICATION DATA

Jones, D. M. (Donald Michael), 1941–
    Tutoring: one to one reading, writing and relating

2nd ed.
ISBN 0-9698010-0-9

1. English language — Rhetoric. 2. Reading.
3. Interpersonal relations. 4. Tutoring of
students. 5. Tutors and tutoring.
I. Title.

PE1408.J65 1994   808'.042   C94-930428-X

EDITOR: James T. Wills
DESIGN: Brant Cowie/ArtPlus Limited
PHOTOGRAPHY: J. Grant Ball

Printed and bound in Canada

Contents

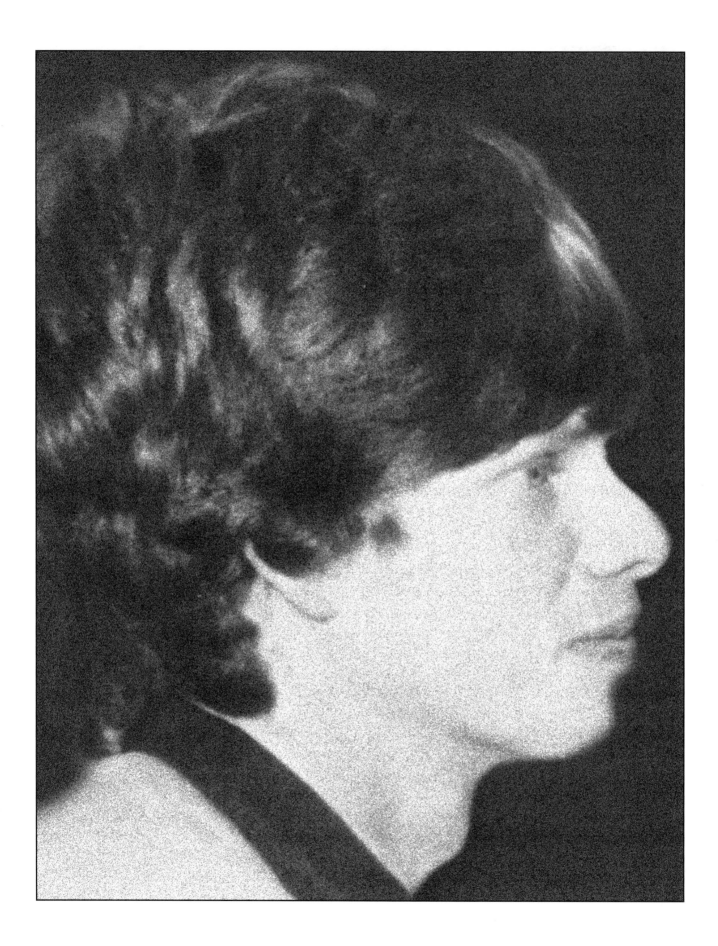

"To Joan, my best pal . . . and to all those educators
I've met who carry this torch and burn it brightly."

PREFACE

SOME STUDENTS HAVE
SEVERE SKILL DEFICIENCIES

STUDENTS HAMPERED IN
THEIR ABILITY TO LEARN

SOME ARE PREDETERMINED
TO FAIL

STUDENTS MAY FEEL
INFERIOR

SUCH STUDENTS NEED
INTENSE DAILY INSTRUC-
TION

The Reading, Writing, and Relating Tutor Program described in this book was developed by the author, primarily because of the significant number of students in the Peterborough area who were entering high school with severe deficiencies in reading and writing skills. Many of these students were reading years below level; a small minority did not read at all.

A large proportion of these students were not able to read many of the texts at grade level, nor were they able to read most unit tests or final exams. Skill-deficient readers were seriously hampered in their ability to learn. Non-readers were often "predetermined" to fail because they were not able to engage printed work.

In frustration, the poor reader will often simply reject academic pursuits, rather than further erode an already poor self-image. Confronted by material that is both unfathomable and the direct cause of feelings of inferiority, the student frequently displays negative behaviour, which, in turn, lessens his or her chances of gaining some degree of literacy.

If these students remain illiterate, not only will they live their lives burdened with feelings of inferiority and resentment, their chance at a meaningful, rewarding future will be severely limited. Fortunately, none of these consequences is necessary, because in almost every case competent, dedicated Reading Tutors will help to raise the reading levels of these students to functional literacy by the time they graduate.

Students who have made little or no progress in reading during eight or more years in school must be provided with intense, saturated, daily instruction if they are to make rapid gains in their final years. The Program, *Tutoring: One-to-One Reading, Writing and Relating* has been developed as a direct response to this need. In my own experience and in the experience of numerous schools across the country, this program has been highly successful, both for the students being tutored and the students acting as tutors. The former benefit from one-to-one attention given by a knowledgeable senior student; the latter gain confidence, solid integrity and the knowledge of just how rewarding helping others to literacy and dignity can be.

TO THE TEACHER

We all share one common goal in education: the opportunity to make a radical, positive and profound difference in the lives of others. Despite our best efforts, some students need a full one-to-one support system on a daily basis. This is something we can't offer. Nevertheless, by working with skilled student colleagues — the tutors described in this book — I have come to realize my educational aspirations. It is my sincere desire that your senior students, and this program, help you achieve yours.

TO THE TUTOR

What can be more rewarding in life than helping another person learn the skills necessary to lead a rewarding life? As a Reading Tutor, you have it in your power to open the world of reading to younger students. Without you, this book would remain closed to them.

TO MY COLLEAGUES

My gratitude to Mary Margaret Thorburn, B. Ed., M.A. (T.E.S.L.), the Program Co-ordinator for the Metropolitan Separate School Board in Toronto. Her chapter on aspects of teaching English to those students for whom English is a second language is an invaluable asset to this text.

My sincere appreciation to Bill Heinmiller, former Math Resource Teacher, and to Brian Neck, Head of Mathematics, for their significant involvement in the preparation of the chapter, *Tutoring in Mathematics*, and to Dr. Michael Peterman for editing it.

DONALD M. JONES

Jan., 1994
Peterborough, Ontario

My Friend

Lisa is my helper.
She forces me to read.
She says to spell out the words
and to say them. She likes it
when I speak English.
If you read, I will give you a break.
She doesn't let me go to the
washroom or get a drunk.
She is a good teacher
She is my friend.
Lisa makes me feel
good.

In February when this little girl in an E.S.L. class gained a tutor, she was experiencing considerable difficulty in school and was still learning her alphabet. She wrote this in May.

One to One Reading, Writing, and Relating

MEET THE NEEDS

THE **R**EADING, **W**RITING, AND **R**ELATING **T**UTOR **P**ROGRAM was conceived and developed as an attempt to meet the needs and maximize the potentials of a significant minority entering secondary school. They are the students who do not read or write well enough to gain the pleasure or academic success they deserve in their final years of school. This program is equally useful in tutoring students for whom English is a second language as well as those at the elementary level who are experiencing difficulty with the basic elements of reading and writing.

ONE-TO-ONE IS THE BEST

Students working together in couples, helping each other in the subject areas, is commonly called Peer Tutoring. That type of activity is a fine way to learn subject work. This program is not that, however. For students with low skills, such an approach would be cosmetic education: a facade. A tutor would be acting simply as a crutch. Your main purpose is to help students gain new and better skills so that they can stand on their own.

ENHANCED SKILLS EQUAL GREATER SUCCESS

Curriculum, or subject work in this course, is of secondary importance. It is a medium for skill growth, not the message, for this is a reading program. All reading and writing should serve the purpose of increasing your student's skills. For example, when writing with your student never, never fall into the trap in which the first draft is your student's and the second or final draft is yours. Type the polished draft, only after you have used writing process with your student. The work must be your student's, if he or she is to improve.

MASTER THE TECHNIQUES

This course is based on the premise that one-to-one instruction is the best of all methods. In it, senior students acting as reading and writing tutors on a daily basis have a unique opportunity. They can help other students gain greater communication skills in one of the most efficient and rapid manners possible as they work under the direction of a classroom teacher.

TEACH READING, WRITING, SUBJECTS AND ACT AS MENTORS/ ROLE MODELS

The positive impact of such gains for your students is far reaching, because once they have enhanced skills, they will be able to obtain

Teaching skills can be very satisfying to tutors.

STUDENTS WANT TO
ENJOY SCHOOL

greater success in their subject areas. Success often results in greater self-esteem and a positive self image. As you know, most students want to obtain both meaning and pleasure from their subject work in school. For some, insufficient skills stand in the way. As a Reading Tutor, you can do much to eliminate such obstacles through a one-to-one relationship with your student. This text is designed to give you basic insights into effective methods currently used by educators to teach reading and writing. Once you have mastered these techniques and are familiar with the materials developed to foster rapid reading growth, you will be well on your way to becoming a capable Reading Tutor.

FULL SPECTRUM OF
SUPPORT NEEDED

Your activities will be multi-faceted. The teaching of reading and writing is the **primary** purpose of this course, but reading tutors also assist their students in subject areas and act as role models and mentors. As such, they become big brothers and sisters to their students, bringing them the full spectrum of support they need for success in school. Through the one-to-one relationship, your students will begin to realize that someone cares, someone takes a personal interest in them. This knowledge will enhance their achievement. Remember, your activities are directed toward the whole student, academically and emotionally. Remember, too, that success breeds success.

Relating is key to learning.

SUCCESS BREEDS SUCCESS

My experience tells me that you may well find being a Reading Tutor one of the most satisfying activities of your years in secondary school. Certainly, many dedicated senior students have already taken pride in the knowledge that their efforts have contributed to the goal of every school: to offer all students the opportunity for a meaningful, rewarding future in tomorrow's society.

BENEFITS AND RESPONSIBILITIES

Many gains, both practical and personal, have been made by reading tutors. However, with these benefits come responsibilities if you expect substantial success.

EXPERIENCE IN HUMAN RELATIONSHIPS

The experience you gain in human relationships is a basic component in many careers. As you work with your student, you will acquire the knowledge necessary to relate effectively with others and understand their needs. In addition to helping others, you will learn to recognize your own self worth and potential for further growth.

Tutors and students work together to produce a class newspaper.

RECOGNIZE YOUR SELF WORTH AND POTENTIAL

Through your work as a Reading Tutor you will learn, in a concrete fashion, how education relates to occupational choices. This, in turn, can help you formulate your own educational plans.

Personal satisfaction is only one of the benefits you can expect. You'll have the special opportunity to interact with students of different backgrounds, abilities and ages as you learn to manage your time effectively and shoulder significant responsibilities.

INTERACT WITH VARIOUS PEOPLE

Tutoring is a program in which you will be working *with non-peer groups*. Within this scenario, you will be involved in the serious, contemporary world issues of literacy and social power. You will have the chance to help improve the lives of others. By designing new techniques, new solutions in teaching reading, you will achieve a very real sense of achievement as you develop your own tailor-made program for your student.

DEAL WITH SERIOUS ISSUES

Personal benefits do not come without significant responsibilities:

• Promptness and regularity in appointments with students.

KNOW THE RECORDS TO MAINTAIN

- Maintenance of specific information on your student's progress for your own teacher, including at least two student profiles per semester (see Appendix A), copies of homework/in-class assignment sheets from teachers, and samples of student's writing progress.

CONTACT SUBJECT TEACHERS

- Keep in regular contact with subject teachers so you can assist students with required assignments and homework.

- Maintain a weekly journal indicating your adherence to the time requirements of this course in order to gain credit, as well as your daily tutoring activities and the progress of students.

ASSIST STUDENT WITH FINAL EXAMS

- Make up an exam schedule with your teacher so you can sit at least one final exam with your student without interfering with your own exams.

READING MANUAL TEST: 75%

- Write and pass a unit test with a grade of 75% on the specifics of this program.

RAPPORT ESSENTIAL

Beyond these requirements, you should work hard to develop a positive rapport with your student in which you demonstrate sensitivity to needs and abilities. Be prepared each day to work with your student on reading, writing and homework/in-class assignments. This includes promoting use of the skills learned by your student in subject courses.

INFORMAL CONFERENCE ONCE PER WEEK

When it seems appropriate, you should be prepared to design specific activities that meet your student's needs.

FORMAL CONFERENCE ONCE PER WEEK

Engage your teacher in a one-to-one, informal conference about your student for about five minutes on a weekly basis. Once a week you should attend a teacher-tutor formal meeting; bring the agenda provided by your teacher, bring your weekly journal, student profiles and notes. Enter your concerns in the "Problems Book," and be prepared to brainstorm problems with the teacher and other tutors.

CONCERNS IN PROBLEMS BOOK

MAINTAIN CONFIDENTIALITY

Your responsibilities also include maintaining absolute confidentiality about the performance levels of your student. However, you should notify the teacher immediately if you suspect any student has difficulties beyond your ability to help, or problems suggesting complex disabilities. Within the first two weeks, tell your students, that most of what you hear from them is for your ears only; however, if anything is said that you believe effects their happiness or well being, you will tell the teacher. While you will always be part of the decision making process, never make a decision about your student in isolation. Finally, implement your teacher's recommendations in a diligent and satisfactory manner.

CHAPTER 2

The Theoretical Framework

ONE-TO-ONE TEACHING
IS THE BEST

STUDENTS HAVE THE
INNATE ABILITY TO READ

SOME MAY NOT VALUE
BOOKS

DEMONSTRATE THE FUN

BOYS 10:1

AGE APPROPRIATE FOR
GIRLS/NOT FOR BOYS

As **A R**eading **T**utor, the degree of success you can expect is based primarily on the benefits of one-to-one teaching. However, a basic understanding of the theory behind teaching reading will assist you to be more effective. This chapter brings you a brief outline of what is otherwise a complex and fascinating field.

There are many reasons why students who have the innate ability to read well don't. Some haven't been read to by their parents when they were children. Consequently, they don't value books and don't realize the enjoyment, pure fun and rewards to be found there. Other students have been assigned books as classroom assignments that have been inappropriate to their interests, development or instructional level. Frequently, teachers of large classes have difficulty responding to the needs or learning pace of the individual reader.

The majority of poor readers is male. Statistics indicate the ratio of male to female may be as high as 10 to 1. There are several hypotheses why this is so. Physically, girls mature earlier than boys. Some psychologists have speculated that girls mature faster than boys in cognition (i.e., the act of thinking). Reading requires abstract thinking. Letters are symbols that stand for thoughts or ideas, and it seems that most girls can master this connection at an earlier age. The result is that while reading assignments may be age-appropriate for girls in primary school they may not be for boys.

Cultural attitudes can have detrimental effects. Reading is often still seen as a passive activity that is appropriate for girls, not boys. This may still be an obstacle for a particular student, but think of your one-to-one relationship as a fresh start.

THE ACT OF READING

GOOD READERS PAY
CLOSE ATTENTION TO
MEANING

It is true that people cannot pay absolute attention to two things at the same time. Reading is a case in point. The reader can either focus on the mechanics of reading (decoding or sounding out), or the meaning. An analogy is learning to drive. Beginners are preoccupied with the mechanics. They are busy steering, signalling, working the clutch, shifting gears. At this stage, no one drives well. Many don't

Student and tutor "lost" in the world of books.

READING PROCESS MUST
BECOME AUTOMATIC

like driving and spend most of their time being nervous and frustrated. Only when the process goes beyond the mechanical and becomes
automatic does the driver have the opportunity for enjoyment.
Reading is similar. The less your student has to attend to the mechanics of reading (phonics), the greater his or her chances to read well
and with pleasure.

Think about yourself. You're a good reader. How do you read? Say
you're curled up in a corner with a terrific book by a favourite author.
At first, you're aware of the book and the words on the page, but as
you slide into a "good read," that changes. You become oblivious to
the mechanics, or even the world around you. Rather than seeing
words, the typical good reader "hears" the characters and "sees" the
setting. At some point, you are not even aware of the book itself.

GOOD READERS BYPASS
MECHANICS

Looked at in this way, it is easy to understand that only when a reader
is completely free from considerations of mechanics is a book read
with ease, enjoyment and, frequently, complete comprehension.

A strictly phonetic approach requires the reader to attend completely
to mechanical decoding. This is not only an obstacle to entering the

EXCLUSIVE PHONICS
APPROACH DIFFICULT

450 PHONIC RULES: WHO
KNOWS THEM ALL?

rich world of reading, it is difficult if not impossible to master. How many phonetic rules do you know without looking them up? Can you list all 450 rules and the 85 exceptions? Don't worry, many good readers can only recall a few. This is not to say that phonics should never be used. Even good readers use phonics on some occasions. The question is to what degree phonics will help.

TEACHING READING SKILLS IN CONTEXT

GOOD READERS DON'T
RELY ON "SOUNDING OUT"

A GOOD GUESS IS BEST

PRIOR KNOWLEDGE IS
ESSENTIAL

A GOOD IDEA OF WHAT A
WORD IS MAKES PHONICS
EASY

IF PHONICS MUST BE
TAUGHT TEACH THEM IN
CONTEXT ONLY

IF YOU KNOW THE WORD,
YOU KNOW THE RULE

In some way, beginning readers must learn the sounds of letters but usually no more than what reading teachers call "survival phonics." Such readers may recognize a word immediately from the initial letters as one in their oral store of language, or they may simply skip it for the time being if recognition is difficult.

If using phonics poses a problem for word interpretation, what's easier? A good guess? Yes, but a *good* guess depends on knowing or having a fairly accurate idea of what the text is all about in the first place. Such prior knowledge stems from the total experience the reader has acquired throughout his or her life. This information has been called pre-reading knowledge, life memory storage, background knowledge or experiential background. One leading reading theorist, Frank Smith, calls this, "non-visual information" and the "theory of the world in our heads" (1979).

That prior knowledge helps in reading can be demonstrated easily. The pronunciation of a word we've never heard can be very difficult if we have to rely exclusively on phonics. However, if we know what a word is likely to be, it is not difficult to confirm or reject a particular pronunciation. As reading teachers know, phonics is easy if you already have a good idea of what the word is in the first place. In fact, it's through such prediction that useful phonics is mastered.

Consider this statement: "The farmer went to the barn to feed hay to the _____." If a student already knows about farms and the animals on them (prior knowledge), then it is relatively easy to predict that the unknown word is likely to be cow, horse or sheep simply by glancing at its initial consonant, not by sounding out the whole word. This is not to suggest that you should totally ignore phonics, but you should teach them in *context* only, and only if necessary.

Again, think about yourself. Consciously, you probably only know ten or so phonetic rules. Even so, as an accomplished reader you know phonic sounds in context. That is, if you know the word, then you know each discrete sound that makes it up. Actually, you have internalized many phonetic rules through whole reading, although you may not know them at a conscious level.

Teaching occasional sounds in context.

EVERYONE HATES DRILL

If it's necessary, point out only when your student is reading that "tion" is always pronounced "shun," that a "y" anywhere in the middle of a word is pronounced "i," as in Clydesdale. Remember everyone hates drills, especially students who have had trouble reading in the past. Actually, only novice readers rely heavily on phonics as a beginning strategy. As readers become more proficient, they become less and less conscious of phonetic rules.

COMPLETE PRIOR
KNOWLEDGE IS BEST

Bear in mind, though, that a student with excellent prior knowledge of a subject will need virtually no instruction in phonics. The student who already knows about work horses will have little trouble pronouncing Clydesdale, particularly if it was mentioned in pre-reading conversation. Teach an occasional phonetic rule in context if necessary, but remember it is probably only necessary because the student's prior knowledge of the subject was incomplete.

Drills and the simple decoding of letter symbols into their respective sounds (phonemes) are weak strategies in the effective teaching of reading. Even if students were able to memorize all the discrete sound symbols in the language (an overwhelming task), they may still only

READING COMPREHENSION IS PARAMOUNT

be able to parrot words without any real understanding of their meanings. In itself, perfect pronunciation is of absolute importance only on the stage. However, reading comprehension is of paramount importance to us all.

THE ROLE OF PREDICTION

READING MUST BE "IN SYNCH" WITH EXPERIENTIAL BASE

Accurate prediction can only occur when the reading material parallels the student's experiential base. This is because the cueing systems of semantics (word meanings) and syntax (word order) allow the student to predict only in a familiar context.

Let's return to our example: "The farmer went to the barn to feed the _____." The semantic (meaning) cues that aid in the correct prediction of the final word are farmer, barn and feed. The syntax (order) cues, which all people who speak English know implicitly, tell the reader that after a verb, "feed," followed by an article, "the," a noun must follow, not another verb, "chuckle," for example, or an adjective like "purple."

SEMANTIC AND SYNTAX QUES ESSENTIAL TO PREDICTION

These syntax and semantic cues alert the reader that the final word is not only a noun, but exclusively an animal noun, more particularly an animal that a farmer feeds in a barn. The initial consonant, "c," confirms the reader's prediction of "cow" and does not require the student to sound out the word. Even so, the student would not be able to use these cues if his or her experiential base did not include agricultural concepts. This very basic example applies to all acts of reading prediction, from the most simple to the most sophisticated. As an adept reader, you are already well equipped to help your students recognize these cues and understand the importance of prediction in successful reading.

CONCEPT MUST BE IN READER'S EXPERIENTIAL BASE

PREDICTION IS THE BEST READING STRATEGY

Prediction is the strongest and most important strategy for building vocabulary and aiding comprehension. Prior knowledge will assist the process. Help your student pick a book at an independent or instructional level that fits his or her experiential base. In short, find out if your student is familiar with a subject before reading starts; familiarity will not only help avoid frustration, but it will act as an aid to comprehension.

BUILD PRIOR KNOWLEDGE BEFORE READING

On the other hand, if a student has little or no prior knowledge of the subject, there are several different techniques that a tutor may use to build necessary concepts before reading begins.

USE PHOTOGRAPHS AND ILLUSTRATIONS

Before starting any book, discuss it with your student. This alone may add to the reader's store of knowledge. He or she may know at least something about the topic, and your conversation may help bring it to a conscious level. Looking at photographs and illustrations (perhaps those in the text to be read), as well as skimming the

The student "investigates" the topic before reading about it.

table of contents and the text itself, will certainly build a student's prior knowledge.

REAL LIFE EXPERIENCES ARE THE BEST

Whenever possible, the best method is to provide real life experiences. One enterprising tutor managed to take her student to a zoo on the weekend before reading a story about zoo animals. The student then wrote about his experience first. This chain of events led to reading not only with enjoyment, but with excellent comprehension. In fact, one of the best ways to learn to read is to write. Writing, after all, is reading one's own words. This is the easiest method of all. As we shall see in a later chapter, writing is one of the primary means used to teach reading to young children.

WRITING IS READING

No matter how the tutor accomplishes the task, the purpose is to prompt and expand a student's prior knowledge of a subject. Only then should reading begin.

"UNDERSTANDING" COMPREHENSION

COMPREHENSION: A
FUNCTION OF PRIOR
KNOWLEDGE

Years ago, I needed an example to illustrate how relatively new theories indicated the manner in which readers comprehend—a difficult task. Common opinion at the time among some audiences seemed to be that comprehension was simply a function of intelligence: people who don't comprehend well when reading just don't think well.

I chose the passage below for them because it was much like the many reading kits that claim to teach reading comprehension. Of course, I tried it before I used it. It would be helpful for you to read it now and attempt the questions on the text before reading further.

A PASSAGE TYPICAL OF
READING KITS

The fuel line is loosened at the primary regulator and the valve on the cylinder for an instant to ensure that there is pressure in the fuel cylinder. Escaping gas can be heard. The fuel line is removed between the primary and secondary regulator (the fuel control). A pressure gauge is attached to the outlet primary regulator, while leaving the gauge connection loose enough to permit a slight leakage of gas. (This will permit an adjustment of the regulator under conditions of actual gas flow.) The top or cap of the primary regulator is taken off.

The fuel cylinder valve is opened and the pressure regulator screw turned in the primary regulator, until a pressure of one and a half pounds is obtained at the pressure gauge. The fuel cylinder valve is turned off, and the cap reassembled. The pressure gauge is removed. The secondary regulator bracket is taken off the carburetor, and the secondary regulator pulled away from the carburetor so that the short rubber fuel line is disconnected. The fuel line between the primary and secondary regulators is assembled. The secondary regulator must remain mounted so that the diaphragm is in a vertical plane.

Questions:
1. Where is the fuel line loosened?
2. Why is the valve on the cylinder opened?
3. What pressure must register on the gauge?
4. When is the pressure gauge removed?

SUCH QUESTIONS DO NOT
TEACH OR MEASURE COM-
PREHENSION

5. Why must a specific pressure be reached in the pressure gauge?
6. For what reason is the top or cap of the primary regulator removed?
7. Evaluate the effect of turning off the fuel cylinder valve before reassembling the cap.
8. Why disconnect the short rubber fuel line rather than the longer line?
9. Hypothesize why the diaphragm is in a vertical plane.
10. What is the purpose and end result of this procedure?

FORTY PERCENT A TYPICAL
SCORE

How did you do? I failed abysmally, although I did manage to answer questions one to four correctly. I can't say I understood the

To evaluate a student's comprehension, establish his or her prior knowledge, then ask questions after the reading is completed.

reading, but I did know where to find these answers in the text. For the balance, it was a different matter, because the remaining questions require some degree of comprehension based on evaluation, inference, and knowledge.

Why did I fail these questions, while the students in a grade ten technical course passed? The point is I had no prior knowledge of the topic, and, therefore, could not comprehend. The only way any non-technical reader could improve the score would be to sit in front of a car engine and increase his or her knowledge of fuel systems as they relate to internal combustion engines.

LACK OF UNDERSTANDING DUE TO POOR PRIOR KNOWLEDGE

Neither you, the tutor, nor your students, should ever feel embarrassed or "stupid" because you do not understand portions of a book. You simply lack sufficient prior knowledge. After all, I failed the technical passage because I have virtually no information in my mental filing cabinet on the internal combustion engine, although I do have many files on the plays of Shakespeare.

NO ONE DOES WELL WITHOUT PRIOR KNOWLEDGE

Our technical example points out that reading an isolated paragraph about a given subject, and then answering the typical ten questions, does little to teach reading comprehension. On the contrary, the effect of such strategies on most poor readers is to frustrate them, embarrass them and, eventually, cause severe feelings of inferiority. After all, who would want to be a consistent "four out of tenner" at any endeavour? Better to say, "I hate reading," and find some other activity that results in a measure of self esteem.

If such strategies do little to teach comprehension, how then do people come to understand the printed word? The question has come under increasingly close scrutiny from psychologists and linguists during the past few decades.

Specialists offer new insights into the very complex matter of reading comprehension, but these insights are themselves correspondingly complex in definition. Therefore, you must pay close attention to the following. Read it more than once if necessary, because this relatively recent information on how the brain processes new concepts or ideas may not be in your experiential base.

A noted expert in the field wrote in the early 1960s that the page of a text contains only the surface structure of meaning (the print), and that the deep structure of meaning (the knowledge of the passage) is actually within the mind of the reader (Chomsky, 1962). In other words, the print is nothing more than squiggles that must be interpreted: letters are symbols for sounds, sounds are symbols for thoughts. Try reading a foreign language. The reader, that is, must bring meaning to the subject: he or she must know at least something about the topic. After all, "Black Holes in Space" meant very little, even to good readers, when the subject was new to the general public.

Piaget, the noted child psychologist, wrote that comprehension is a process of assimilation and accommodation that results in a shift in cognitive or thinking structures. This is quite a mouthful, but the truth of it is shown by the following example. A person reads an editorial from one newspaper on a given subject, thereby gaining one point of view on a topic. However, if the same person reads or assimilates a number of editorials from various newspapers on the same subject, it is likely that his or her perceptions would alter to accommodate opposing points of view.

Most tutors are aware of the term "metaphor" from regular English classes. It is a means of expressing one thing in terms of another, but it is not a literal description. "My love is a red, red rose." Here, the loved one is compared to the rose in a metaphor that brings to mind all the connotations of that lovely flower: beauty, fragility, softness and perhaps even the pain associated with its thorns.

Long before the linguists and psychologists expounded on how the brain processes information, poets were involved in the question. Robert Frost, for example, wrote simply, "We learn by metaphor." It might be said, then, that acquiring new knowledge

EMBARRASSING FOR THOSE WHO DO NOT DO WELL

CONSISTENT POOR PERFORMANCE MAKES STUDENTS DETEST READING

SURFACE STRUCTURE ON THE PAGE

DEEP STRUCTURE IN READER'S MIND

READER MUST BRING MEANING TO TEXT

ASSIMILATION/ ACCOMMODATION EQUALS NEW LEARNING

WE LEARN BY METAPHOR

Discuss stories before they are read.

ANALOGY BRIDGES
THE GAP

STEPPING STONES TO
COMPREHENSION IN
EXPERIENTIAL BASE

TRANSFER OF LEARNING

takes place by the comparison of the known with the new. Our minds enumerate the similarities and differences as a direct aid to comprehending the new with the aid of metaphor. In this view, the stepping stones to our comprehension of new information are imbedded in our experiential base.

Piaget's theories can be illustrated by a number of examples. Knowing how to ride a bicycle, a familiar skill to many people, will assist an individual to ride a motorcycle. In the same way, knowing how to play tennis helps a great deal in other racquet sports. Such a transfer of learning to new situations is the essence of reading comprehension.

More directly related to your development as a Reading Tutor is an experiment I conducted at the University of Toronto. A number of educators were in the process of obtaining their Specialist Certification in Reading. Initially, each candidate was given a protractor to jog his or her memory of its function: marking angles between 0 and 360 degrees. Then they were able to apply this knowledge (a concept in their experiential base) to discover the function of an engineer's transit: essentially a sophisticated protractor fixed on a tri-

Tutor increases her student's prior knowledge.

THIS IS LIKE THAT

pod. As Frost said, "We learn by metaphor (Your teacher will tell you we learn by similie: he or she is perfectly correct!)."

The critical step in building prior knowledge was having the teachers use a protractor beforehand. This tactic allowed them to tap their experiential base for protractor-like objects. Without this technique, the experiment stood little chance of success.

What this entire theoretical chapter implies is that your ability to comprehend, and more importantly, that of your students, is enhanced through real or vicarious experiences of the world. Viewing, reading, and listening all contribute to the experiential base. Someone may have a very fine brain, but a lack of specific information stored on a given topic limits or seriously hampers the brain's ability to comprehend.

STUDENTS' ABILITY TO COMPREHEND THE PRINTED WORD CAN INCREASE

ENSURE READERS HAVE ADEQUATE PRIOR KNOWLEDGE

All readers must have some prior knowledge of a topic in their experiential base. A crucial part of your task as a Reading Tutor is to help your student comprehend what is read. Use the concepts outlined here to ensure that you activate and increase your students' prior knowledge so they can relate any new ideas they encounter to the information they already possess.

CHAPTER 3

Teaching Successful Reading

THE **PREVIOUS CHAPTER** discussed reading and comprehension from a theoretical standpoint. Here we will be looking at the methods that will help you fulfil your role as a Reading Tutor from a practical perspective.

LEARNING STYLES

VARIOUS STYLES OF LEARNING

In recent years, teachers have become much more aware that individual students have a preferred method or style of learning. Some learn best by hearing, others by seeing, still others by doing.

Reflect for a moment, and you will be able to determine your own preference. This personal exercise will help you determine how your students like to learn. Alternately, ask the teacher for a Learning Styles Inventory Test. Whatever the preferred method, use it frequently. It has the greatest potential for easy, rapid and significant gains. However, don't use it exclusively, because the only way to strengthen your student's other learning styles is by working with them.

LEARNING STYLES INVENTORY TEST

LEARNING BEST BY SEEING

LEARNING BEST BY HEARING

"HANDS-ON" LEARNING

If a student learns best by seeing, view the film of a novel before you begin reading. Having a careful look at photos or illustrations is a good pre-reading activity as well. On the other hand, if a student's strength is hearing, use a listen and read format with novels so that your student hears the words as he or she sees them. Do the same with scripts: allow the student to hear all the roles as they are read. Someone who learns by doing should be encouraged to act out scripts or plots. Alternately, have students write their own scripts and then take roles. As they gain proficiency in these approaches, try to touch on all learning styles during lessons.

GLOBAL/ANALYTIC LEARNING

Beyond these preferred styles of learning, there are students who learn "globally;" they understand the big picture. They should read through a script or story with very little interruption until the very end. Once they have captured the major ideas or themes, you can review the details of plot, character and sequence to aid in comprehension. Still others learn analytically; they need the details of plot, character, theme and sequence pointed out to them from scene to scene or chapter to chapter in order to comprehend the whole reading.

The Reading Room should be one in which students can be relaxed and spontaneous.

As you work with your students, these preferred learning styles will become more and more clear, but it is important to bear these distinctions in mind from the very beginning.

THE READING ROOM

THE READING ENVIRON-
MENT IS IMPORTANT

Even though your attitudes, knowledge and abilities are paramount in helping the learning reader, the physical makeup of the reading environment can either enhance or decrease a student's opportunity for significant gains. The Reading Room must be a place where your students can make "mistakes" without fear of criticism or embarrassment, a place where they can feel relaxed and spontaneous. Statistics indicate that many students don't read well because they are poor risk takers. They won't take a chance on a new word, so in short, they don't progress in vocabulary and word concepts. Making them feel safe and secure is the first step in helping them take these necessary risks.

STUDENTS MAY BE
POOR RISK TAKERS

TUTORS ARE BIG BROTH-ERS/BIG SISTERS

You will be in a good position to begin this process. For the most part, you will be near in age to your students. Often, you will share the same interests, attitudes and enthusiasms. With young children, the fact that you are a teenager will be a benefit. Tutors work one-to-one, and you will have a greater opportunity to make a maximum positive impact than if you had to work with large numbers. This relationship is not unlike that of a big brother or big sister. As a positive role model, you can turn a reluctant learner around by dispelling the negative attitudes created by past frustrations and failures.

STRONG BONDS CAN FORM

Usually, the tutor-student relationship is satisfying to both participants. A strong bond can be formed, and this can form the chemistry for a positive environment where tutor and student settle into a private world of their own.

LOTS OF DIFFERENT BOOKS ARE NEEDED

The Reading Room should contain a full spectrum of reading materials—from pictorial magazines to comic books, from exciting paperbacks to classic novels embedded with rich and colourful language. The emphasis should be on various reading levels and themes. With such an array, a student will soon learn to exercise freedom of choice. In a tutoring environment, in fact, there should be no other authority who says, "This is fine literature. You must read and enjoy it," or alternately, "Don't read this. It's inappropriate and uninteresting."

STUDENTS MUST DECIDE WHAT IS INTERESTING

The reader should be the judge of what is appropriate or interesting, difficult or easy according to his or her unique perspective and development. This is the reason that novels of many types and formats have a place in the Reading Room, including the "High Interest/Low Vocabulary" novels that many students favour. The themes of these books cater to the adolescent, they appear in an adult format, but they are actually written at a lower level than many books for teenagers. Reading well from such books will give a student the confidence to try more challenging works at a later stage.

STUDENTS NEED TO DEVELOP CONFIDENCE

If your student doesn't like such books, you might try the paperbacks that should be part of the Reading Room stock. Often, these are written at or below an adult level. You might even try contemporary novels. Some analyses indicate that much of Hemingway and Steinbeck are at a "low" vocabulary level, although obviously they do not measure the concepts contained in the writing.

AVOID FRUSTRATION THRESHOLD

No matter how you begin, once a student has gained confidence, he or she should be encouraged to move on to other reading levels, always avoiding the "**frustration threshold**." Reading really is a developmental process. As a student develops reading skills and, consequently, an interest in literature, he or she will value the opportunity to delve into all kinds of reading. That's why a "paperback spinner" or two with a whole range of novels and tables laden with magazines and books are an integral part of the Reading Room.

"LISTEN AND READ" FORMAT FOR DIFFICULT NOVELS

Feel free to bring your own favourites if students appear receptive. If a novel is well above the individual student's level, use a "listen and read" approach in which the tutor reads aloud and the student follows silently. This strategy allows students to encounter texts many years above their independent reading level but not beyond their oral comprehension. If students are given final choice over the books they read, their tastes and skills should develop to the point that they value the books treasured by tutors and teachers alike.

STUDENTS GIVEN FINAL CHOICE LEARN TO VALUE BOOKS

An example may help. One senior level tutor who was very fond of the novel, *Lord of the Flies,* described it to his student, and they read it together using a listen and read format. Although the student had been defined upon entry to secondary school as a "grade two reader," near the end of the tutoring program he was able to read the opening passages of this Pulitzer Prize winning novel to an appreciative Board of Education. Proud student! Proud tutor!

GUIDING LIGHTS TO SUCCESSFUL READING

RELAX AND RELATE

INDEPENDENT TO INSTRUCTIONAL LEVEL OF READING

ACTIVATE PRIOR KNOWLEDGE

Don't begin reading until both you and your student are relaxed and relating. At first, help the student find a book at his or her independent level, then, as he or she gains confidence, move on to the instructional level. This can be determined by asking the teacher or completing a Reading Level Analysis of the text to be read. As discussed in Chapter 2, activate and build your student's prior knowledge of a topic.

Teach phonics only in context. This approach will be unnecessary if the student's prior knowledge has been prepared adequately. If the student has trouble, assist the prediction process by sounding a word's initial consonants. Floundering over a word for more than a few seconds indicates the reader should skip it. Just say, "We'll talk about that one later," rather than allowing endless attempts to sound out an unfamiliar word. This can lead to embarrassment and frustration. However, if skipping distorts the meaning or slows the reading, give the student the word.

EMOTIONAL BONDING NECESSARY

The books chosen should be capable of making your student laugh or even cry. By the age of thirteen many non-readers hate reading, and such books will provide emotional interest and bonding between tutor and student.

When you are reading orally and the student is following silently, **make sure your student's eyes are on the same line of type.** Read with enthusiasm, expression and at a speed the student can follow. You can probably read at more than 200 words per minute, but those who read with difficulty may often be lost above 50 to 100 words per minute.

BE AWARE OF STUDENT'S READING SPEED

Don't allow your student to read with a finger as a word guide. This indicates that he or she is focusing too closely on the mechanics of phon-

Learning must be a joyful game!

WHEN NECESSARY PROVIDE SEE-THROUGH RULER

ics, and you must break the habit. Bear in mind that some words depend exclusively on context for identification, as in "I played the record," or "I will record the information." If necessary, provide a see-through ruler as a word guide so the reader can see context clues ahead of time.

READING MUST BE FUN!

Watch your student closely, because to succeed it is essential to stop the session before the student becomes frustrated or extremely tired. When the reading is finished for the day, make sure you demonstrate that you understand just how much effort reading requires from discouraged students. Ensure your praise is genuine for genuine effort and accomplishment. Most importantly, make reading a joyful game as you follow the basic principles of success listed below.

THE PRINCIPLES OF READING SUCCESS

GET TO KNOW EACH OTHER

1. At the first session with your student, just get to know something about each other.

BE AWARE OF READING
LEVELS

2. Ensure that you are aware of your student's independent, instructional and frustrational reading levels. (Check with the teacher.)

INDEPENDENT LEVEL FIRST

3. During your initial sessions, make sure that all books read are at your student's independent level. When your student reads well for you, he or she will quite probably feel good about the program and rapport usually develops as a consequence.

TEACH AT INSTRUCTIONAL
LEVEL

4. Work at developing the student's trust.

5. Once trust and respect are mutual, move on to your student's instructional level (the growth level) of reading.

6. Check that all texts used to develop your student's reading ability are at his or her instructional level (Check with your teacher to find out the method of evaluation).

7. Always perceive your student in need of skill growth, rather than at a low intellectual level or perceptually handicapped. Your job is not to be a diagnostician, but simply to teach reading.

8. Treat your student respectfully as an equal human being.

DEVELOP RAPPORT

9. Trust and security enhance reading progress. Develop a close rapport with your student by using these techniques:

— relax with your student by engaging briefly in casual conversation

— explore mutual interests

— appreciate your student's efforts and accomplishments in a genuine way

— laugh once in a while, shared humour is contagious

— reinforce only genuine effort and accomplishments with praise.

10. Become aware of your student's strengths and weaknesses. Use the strengths to reduce the weaknesses.

AVOID ULTIMATUMS

11. Be sensitive to verbal and non-verbal messages.

YOU ARE A ROLE MODEL

12. Avoid ultimatums and an authoritarian stance; use natural and logical consequences.

13. Remember that you are an important role model.

SET STANDARDS

14. Be flexible in your approach to teaching reading. People, after all, are individuals who respond to different methods.

15. Be consistent by setting fair, firm and effective standards for behaviour and conduct during your lessons. Identify and concentrate together on the task at hand.

16. Remember to relate prior knowledge to the reading topic before your student begins to read.

17. Listen to what your student has to say and respond appropriately.

18. Never speak down to students or use language that is not age appropriate.

OPPORTUNITIES FOR SUCCESS

19. Ensure that your tutor-student sessions have lots of opportunity for success by letting the student select topics, make choices, suggest assignments.

20. Always strive to increase your student's skill level, but at the same time be patient and encouraging. Remember, it may have taken you at least ten years to become a competent reader.

21. Be positive and enthusiastic throughout your sessions.

BELIEVE IN YOUR STUDENT

22. Believe your student can and will improve; by osmosis he or she will begin to believe it too.

23. Be prepared. Know exactly what is expected of you before your tutorial session begins. If you are not certain, consult your teacher.

24. Be yourself. Use your personality to make the student-tutor connection.

25. Be a student-watcher: evaluate and revise your plans based on your student's response.

USE SELF-EVALUATION

26. Remember that self-evaluation is the most useful type of evaluation for both you and your student.

27. Consult the teacher immediately whenever a problem arises, or you need clarification.

28. Enjoy the lesson periods, see them as worthwhile no matter how much or how little is accomplished. See yourself as an effective Reading Tutor who will make a positive difference in your student's life.

BE A GOOD BUDDY

29. Try to be a good buddy and mentor to your student. When warranted, attempt to be his or her advocate. Everyone in this world needs someone else to stand beside them!

CHAPTER 4

Techniques and Materials for Rapid Reading Growth

EVEN BEYOND THE METHODS we have looked at, there are additional techniques that will assist you to help your students read better quickly. Once you have mastered them, you can move on to select the materials that your students find most appropriate and interesting at their particular levels.

WORD-PROMPT WHEN NECESSARY

Reading and Following. In the first of these fundamental techniques, the student reads orally while you follow silently, prompting when necessary. This assumes that the student knows most words in the material being read. In the second method, the Reading Tutor reads, while the student follows silently. Be sure to watch your speed here, keeping to 50 to 75 words per minute for the first while.

SIMULTANEOUS READING

Choral Reading. In this strategy, you and your student read orally and simultaneously. Your voice should be considerably louder than your student's, but, again, be careful with your speed.

STUDENT ECHOES TUTOR'S READING

Echoic or Impress Reading. When using this technique, you should read relatively faster than in preceding methods. The student should read the same word just split seconds behind you as you direct your voice toward the student's ear.

When using Choral or Echoic Reading, do not correct the student's errors, because you are striving for speed and attempting to facilitate comprehension.

SOUND INITIAL CONSONANTS ONLY

Student Reads, Tutor Sounds. This strategy is primarily for students who read few or no words. As the student reads orally, softly sound beginning or initial consonants of virtually every word. Allow the student to predict the balance of the word, thus lessening his or her frustration while adding speed.

Listen and Read Tapes. Occasionally, record "listen and read tapes" of the student's own stories or subject readings and assign them as homework.

Reading should be fun!

APPROPRIATE READING MATERIAL

FRY'S ANALYSIS TO
DETERMINE TEXT
READING LEVEL

You can be the best trained tutor in the world, but your student may graduate unable to read the word"diploma" unless reading materials are appropriate. They must be at the student's independent and instructional levels and be enjoyable. On a regular basis, each student should be reading a different book at an appropriate level based on that student's richness of language and experience. To accelerate a student's reading ability rapidly, some form of listen and read format should be used, such as one or all of the following: high interest/ low vocabulary novels, collective novel study, or film, play and television scripts.

EXPERIENCE STORY
MAXIMIZES OPPORTUNITY
FOR SUCCESSFUL
PREDICTION

As we have seen in earlier chapters, the strongest reading strategy for word knowledge and comprehension is prediction. This occurs most successfully when the reader's prior knowledge is in concert with the passages to be read. Your student will have an immediate measure of success when reading his or her own story in his or her own words.

Experience Stories. To begin, ask your student to tell you a story about something he or she did after school or on a weekend. Sports, games, trips, viewing films are all good subjects.

CORRECT ONLY WHEN MEANING IS DISTORTED

Copy the student's words exactly, and try to print for easy reading. Then ask your student to read the experience story back to you immediately, before memory fade starts to erode prediction ability. Don't correct errors unless the word read does not fit the context. "Mistakes" when reading are not errors, they are **miscues**. If the student reads "ate" for "swallowed" (phonetically dissimilar), it is probably fine for the sense of the passage. However, "The cat swabbed the goldfish" for "The cat swallowed the goldfish," despite the phonetic similarity, is not and should be corrected by you. When the miscue fits the meaning, as in "ate," it is called **positive**. When it distorts meaning, as in "swabbed," it is **negative** and should be pointed out to the student.

POSITIVE MISCUES

NEGATIVE MISCUES

Ask your student to copy the experience story into his or her book as writing practice, but you might also enter it on the word processor after it has been written out by hand to give it a more "professional" look. As the number of these stories grows, file them in a folder. By the end of the year the student will have the equivalent of a novel, an excellent way to generate self esteem and confidence through accomplishment.

SCRIPTS: HIGHLY MOTIVATIONAL

Scripts. Film and television scripts are always popular with students. You can assist your students by having them rehearse roles for group script reading. You might play a number of roles while they play theirs, but make sure your students follow as you read your parts orally. Tell them they must follow so they will know their cues.

EMPLOY NATURAL SPEAKING PATTERNS

Scripts are excellent for fostering reading ability for a number of reasons. They motivate: many of the characters are admired or even idolized by students. Students will gain genuine vicarious enjoyment by playing the characters they admire. Scripts are natural: the dialogue is often written in real life speech patterns—the easiest language for students to read. Scripts are familiar: many film and television shows have been seen time and time again, so students are able to approach the reading with prior knowledge of plot, theme and content, which promotes comprehension.

OFFER ADVANCE KNOWLEDGE OF PLOT AND THEME

'LISTEN AND READ' FORMAT ELICITS RAPID GROWTH

Scripts help avoid a phonics approach. The effect of a number of students and Reading Tutors reading orally while the remainder of the students follow silently has the same positive effect as listen and read tapes. Laborious and often inaccurate phonics-based guesses are bypassed, and vocabulary growth will be enhanced by hearing other students pronounce the words. Reading speed also will be increased, enhancing the ability to enjoy and understand the material.

THEMES CONTEMPORARY AND SIMPLISTIC

Screen plays encourage a positive attitude to reading in the mind of the reluctant reader, because generally they have broad appeal and contemporary themes. Overall, students are very aware and interested

This student exudes confidence even with a book almost as big as herself!

INTENSE PROMOTION BY
FILM COMPANIES

in new film and television scripts due to the intense promotion generated by the companies producing them.

Novels for Low Level Readers. Some novels are designed specifically for high school students with extremely low reading levels. The themes and characters are created to hold the interest of this group. Even so, because the language has been stripped to the basics, these stories give students only minimal opportunities to practice the crucial skill of predicting. Use such books sparingly and only to build confidence in fledgling readers. Read them with as much expression as you can muster, because although these students might read at lower levels, they speak at the grade level they attend. A flat oral delivery can only be tedious.

TEENAGE THEMES AT
INDEPENDENT/INSTRUC-
TIONAL LEVELS

STUDENT'S SPEAKING
LEVEL MUCH HIGHER
THAN READING LEVEL

As soon as you feel your students are ready, assist them to find other paperbacks that are written at their instructional level. There are literally thousands of paperbacks that don't signal "low learner." You'll find

MANY PAPERBACKS AT INSTRUCTIONAL LEVELS

these titles in the Reading Room or on many library shelves. Not only are the topics exciting, they use language closer to your student's speaking level.

One excellent method of promoting this type of advancement is to find an opportunity to take students to a "book bargain" warehouse. Shopping carts at the ready, you and your student can take away books for as little as $1 to $2 each. The self-image gains are well worth the effort, and such a trip is one sure way to increase your student's "ownership" of language and reading.

DEAL WITH ISSUES IMPORTANT TO TEENS

Bibliotherapy Units. These paperbacks tend to deal with issues that preoccupy teens. They might dwell on parents who appear to hate your boyfriend or girlfriend, loyalty, abuse, danger, learning to grow up, learning to love, developing responsibility and so on. These books may reveal to students that they are not alone with their problems and might encourage them to talk. Consult a librarian to find out about popular authors who write for teenagers.

SOMETHING FOR EVERYONE

Newspapers. Papers are effective teaching tools because they are highly pictorial and have something of interest for everyone. Written at grade two and grade three levels for new immigrants, *Newcomer News* is provided free by the government. Some regular newspapers are written at a very low level according to analyses of basic language, ideas and photographic content.

MAGAZINES ARE A FINE MEDIUM FOR BUILDING READING SKILLS

Magazines. Don't forget to make use of the many magazines and, yes, even comic books to be found in the Reading Room. Contribute to the student's sense of "ownership" of language and reading by asking him or her to bring in a favourite. Popular magazines contain innumerable one to two page interviews and profiles of current film idols and rock stars.

DRIVER'S MANUAL A MUST

Driver's Manuals. There comes a time in the hearts of all teenagers when the desire to obtain a driver's licence is all consuming. The only way to do that is to read and understand the manual. Enough said! These manuals are provided free at both an adult and grade four level by government highway departments. Encourage your student to write the tests included. Advancement in comprehension is one benefit. Getting the licence is the incentive.

Anything! Use anything your student has a desire to read, provided it isn't at his or her frustration level. If you suspect it is, employ the read and follow technique discussed before.

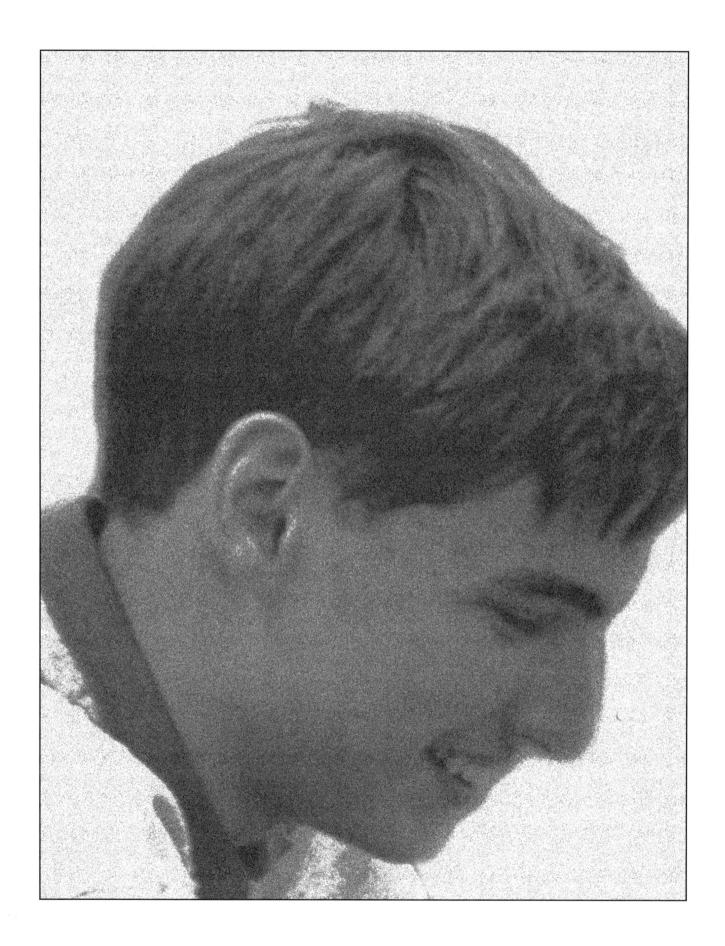

Teaching Writing

WRITING IS ONE OF THE BEST METHODS of communication precisely because the nature of the process allows us the time and scope for maximum creativity, self-expression, reflection and revision. That's why so many children enjoy writing: not only is it creative, but it's their "own stuff." Just as in reading, a safe environment for risk-taking is essential for writing to develop. Your students should feel confident in expressing their feelings, in experimenting, without fear of intervention and censure.

Some primary school children are so enthralled with their stories that they won't even go out for recess until they're finished. Blissfully unaware of spelling and structural rules, these children write from a wellspring of feelings and ideas. One young child described her cat: "Mi kt iz pte. Sye is org an gra!" (My cat is pretty. She is orange and grey.) She wasn't afraid to try words like "centipede" or "catastrophe," either. This lack of inhibition made for terrific, authentic writing. It arose from a classroom environment that gave ownership (choice of topic and format) to the student. If you strive for the same type of conditions, teaching writing can be a successful, rewarding exercise for students and tutors alike.

William Shakespeare was a terrific writer, but he wasn't much on spelling. In fact, in one play he spelled the word "sky" four different ways. "Creative spelling" was the norm until Dr. Samuel Johnson wrote his definitive dictionary in the eighteenth century. His work effectively standardized spelling, and after that people began to be more concerned with it. Nevertheless, even as late as the nineteenth century the English author Charles Dickens was known to be less than consistent in spelling when writing his novels.

The point is that spelling is a function of writing, not the other way around. Great literature often follows the convention of standardized spelling, but not always, and the importance of the words on the page is not changed.

This is true for many of your students. They are frequently much more concerned with spelling conventions than the act of writing. Standards of spelling and form act as censors on their natural desire to communicate by writing. As the most skill-deficient students, often they have found the most red marks on their assignments in the past.

This student expresses his thoughts with no fear of censure.

WRITING IS FAR MORE THAN JUST SPELLING AND CURSIVE WRITING ABILITY

Over the years, these scars have made them very vulnerable and inhibited, turning them into people who think they will always fail. Simply put, they equate writing with spelling and cursive writing ability. To return to Dickens once more, a brief glance at one of his manuscripts shows that his pen hand was not good—but his novels are brilliant. As Reading Tutors, it is your job to break down these fears and inhibitions in your students, unlock their creativity, and help them express their thoughts.

WRITING IS EXPLORATIVE/TENTATIVE

Years ago, schools encouraged two basic confusions about writing. First, writing was taught in a fragmented manner, something learned sequentially, with rigid rules of composition that could be formulated and charted. Second, the thought was that people should write what was already completely formulated in their minds. Writing, therefore, had to be "perfect" from the start. As we know now, writing is explorative, tentative and personal. The time to get out the dictionary and check spelling—as we must—is when we are ready to *"publish."* Form alone, without the sparkle of intellect, is stale at best and drivel at worst.

SPELLING IS LEARNED THROUGH CONSTANT READING/WRITING

Many students can't spell because they haven't had the practice. The old saying is: "You can't do it unless you do it." Think about it. No one plays tennis perfectly from the very first. It's the same with spelling. Your students haven't engaged in constant, repetitive reading and writing; the kind of practice that builds "word pictures" or mind images of how words are spelled. Unlike you and me, these students have not had the opportunity to internalize the basic concepts contained in various forms and styles of writing.

STUDENTS AFRAID TO TAKE RISKS

Inhibitions created in the past will lead students to choose the simplest of words, much below their oral level of language. They won't risk the word "centipede" when they can play it safe with "ant." Even so, many have a marvellous potential for writing well. Despite their fear about word selection, students at the secondary level possess language skills far richer and more sophisticated than those of very young children. As well, their fund of experience, or prior knowledge, is much more advanced. What we need to do is deprogram the beliefs that spelling is the same as writing and that there are no intermediate stages (revision and editing) between writing and publishing.

ORAL LANGUAGE IS RICH

ASSIST STUDENTS TO DEVELOP THEIR OWN "VOICE" IN WRITING

When you think about it, writing is a form of speaking on paper. There are conventions, of course, that differ from spoken language, and these must be learned and practiced. However, listen creatively to one of your students telling you about something keenly felt. Then consider how you can help that student put the richness of that personal "voice" into writing. As a Reading Tutor, you can help your students make dramatic gains in writing in a relatively short time. Simply accept that they have the *ability*; all they need is a safe environment in which to write their "own stuff."

RECORD STUDENT'S ORAL LANGUAGE

Some junior students in higher academic levels read well but have comparatively low writing skills. They may need exclusive writing tuition one or two days per week. Their oral language may be fluent, but their writing can appear stilted, lacking coherence and flow. Writing is not simply written down oral language, but one beginning strategy is to tape the student's spoken words and then have him or her transcribe them line by line. Because the student's oral language is appropriate from both a syntactical and semantic point of view, the transcribed speech will be too. After a number of sessions, the effect of copying this modelling of oral language will bring your student insights into the mechanics of clear writing.

USE WRITING PROCESS

Overall, keep this very general procedure for teaching writing in mind as you tutor your student: think/ tell/ discuss/ write/ discuss/ read/ rewrite. Following this path may lead either to a final, polished draft or, at least, to one that pleases the writer. Don't forget, though, that a project leading nowhere can simply be abandoned in favour of more profitable pursuits.

STUDENT'S MARK SHOULD BE BASED ON IMPROVEMENT

Your student should be given lots of praise for real effort, but only one mark for writing. Award it at the end of term. Most, if not all, of this mark should be based on his or her degree of improvement over time. When marking, be sure to apply individual standards, rather than absolutes; a much more fair, beneficial and realistic method for all students. If available, use benchmarks or educational standards for evaluation which are samples of student performance at different levels. These may be available in your school.

THE TUTOR'S ROLE

ENGAGE IN NATURAL DIALOGUE

A NUMBER OF DRAFTS FOR "PUBLISHED" WRITING

WRITERS ARE PROUD OF FINE WORK!

AUTHENTIC TOPICS CAN PRODUCE COPIOUS WRITING

The whole key to these pre-writing and "during writing" activities is to engage in a very natural dialogue with the student concerning the topic at hand. Don't worry about time. As the student's personal tutor, your job is not to amass sheer volumes of scribbles over the term but to assist your student in producing a lot of "writing process" writing. Quantity of this latter type eventually leads to quality. Writing involves lots of thinking, talking and, of course, a number of drafts for any piece of writing that will be "published (When someone else will read it)."

One senior tutor who was in his final year of school became very good friends with his student, a boy of thirteen. They had a common denominator in their lives: a love of fishing. They discussed the incidents of a shared fishing experience at length, some of which must have been very humorous judging by the laughter. Then the student began to write. With much discussion and many suggestions, it was a full two weeks before the final, polished draft was completed. Nevertheless, in his previous school career the boy had never written anything longer than half a page. The story of his fishing trip was twenty-three pages long! Furthermore, it was a fine story, one that both his tutor and teacher enjoyed reading. The writer was proud of such epic work! Authentic topics, personally felt, produce copious writing.

CONFERENCING—A CRUCIAL SKILL

CONFERENCING PROMPTS AND FOCUSES WRITING

LISTEN CREATIVELY

YOUR QUESTIONS CAN HELP STUDENTS INTERNALIZE THE WRITING PROCESS

Conferencing with your student will help prompt and focus writing. While your student will need private time to write on occasion and, indeed, will produce private writing for his or her eyes only, you are there at all times to collaborate in the writing when needed. By using creative listening and receiving the student's writing positively, you can help him or her learn all the drafting stages and processes involved in writing a polished piece. Make only a few suggestions. Introduce your remarks with something like: "I need more information about _____," or "What colour was it?" and "I enjoyed the way you said _____."

Conferencing before work begins.

PRAISE FROM "INNER
VOICE" THE BEST!

What you, the tutor, want for your student is a growing awareness that he or she is capable of obtaining legitimate success in writing. You see, the student must have a sense of personal accomplishment, for that is the only way he or she will begin to enjoy writing. ***External praise can never do as much as that little voice inside one's own head can: "This is good and I did it."*** By simple statements like: "I need more information about _____; I liked the way you said _____." you are helping your student experiment with description and accuracy of word-pictures.

ONE-TO-ONE

TUTORS OFFER FULL
SUPPORT

The real advantage of one-to-one assistance is that poor writers feel more free to use the richness of their own language without fear. You are always there to sympathize, support, spell on final drafts and define words to help maintain writing flow. This kind of closeness promotes writing growth. When students are finally free from worries about spelling and composition form, they have the freedom to go anywhere in writing that their intellect and imagination can take them. In the end, spelling ability and composition form improve automatically through constant writing and revision.

STRATEGIES FOR SUCCESSFUL WRITING

Fluency or Copious Writing: "Lots of Stuff." One of the easiest ways to establish a flow of words on paper is to play a game with your student that Peter Elbow described as "Freewriting," 1981. Each of you scribble away on your own paper as fast as you can without paying attention to spelling, your pen hand or word choice. The point is not to stop. When the game finishes, the student shows you the page for a "two second flip." This way he or she won't be embarrassed by the appearance of the writing, because you won't really see it long enough to comment or form an opinion. The object of freewriting is to lose inhibitions and learn to write by doing. The student can write anything, even repetitions of the same words, until new ideas come to mind. This is much like the "Listening Games" discussed in Chapter 8. Freewriting helps the student write in a style that approximates automatic and effortless speech. Some psychologists call this mind-hand-paper link kinetic memory in which "the moving hand always writes." Freewriting doesn't allow the writer time to stew over spelling, rules or form, which may interrupt his or her thoughts, and, hence, writing flow.

Freewriting Modes. Change the rules of the game occasionally. Write dialogue for plays developed by you and your student. You write a line, then your student responds with the next. Say it, then write it

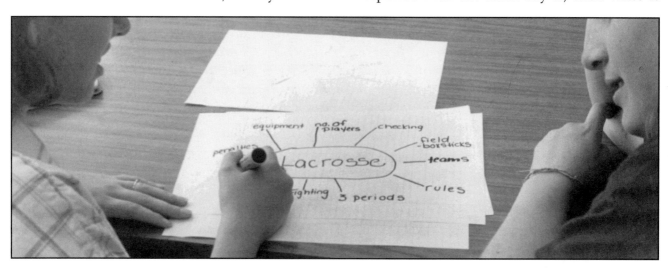

A tutor initiates writing with a "thought web".

immediately. Each one of you responds directly to what the other has said. The dialogue will, consequently, shape and reshape the plot.

Thought Webs. This strategy is useful when your student feels there is little to write on a topic. Draw a bubble on paper that contains the main topic; hockey, for example. Discuss the topic with your student and draw spokes from the bubble that point to such associated ideas as game rules, equipment, various plays and the names of hockey stars. Once a series of spokes has been added, the student will have sufficient information to write at length.

Topic Selection. Writers have to have topics. They're everywhere: in memory, reading, viewing, listening, dialogue and, certainly, the products of the creative imagination. If a student seems to be suffering from memory block, ask for a long list of everything he or she knows something about. A topic is bound to come out.

Writing is a dynamic process. It undergoes constant changes as a person reads, thinks, dialogues and rewrites. One has only to view the multiple drafts of authors like Charles Dickens and other great writers to see the truth of this statement. Often, writers don't know what they truly think about a given topic until after they write a first draft. The best thinking, then, is forged through writing.

Methods vary, but there is a general procedure that many writers appear to experience. Your students will probably be the same. The writer must have sufficient time to think of potential topics, because no one can write, immediately, in a vacuum. After deliberation, your student should choose the one topic he or she likes most, the one he or she can complete best.

Before writing begins, it is often a good idea for your student to tell you the whole story to bring it fully and vividly to mind. Of course, if you appear to enjoy the story, make positive comments and demonstrate real interest, you will do much to motivate your student. Assist with clarity by asking questions and perhaps prompting the student to expand the story: "Why did that happen?" or "I don't understand this part." Also, you might make suggestions for additions or deletions in a positive, unthreatening way. Appropriately couched comments might be: "What do you think if you included this?", or "I really like this part; will you keep it in?" and "Tell me what this means." Then ask, "What's next?"

All these questions and comments must be phrased so that control of the writing remains with the writer. When ownership of the project stays with the student, with no overseer, then he or she maintains authority over the writing. This leads to students who don't have to wait for someone to tell them what to write, uninhibited students who internalize the process your questions suggest.

THOUGHT WEBS FURTHER DEVELOP WRITING TOPICS

TOPICS ARE EVERYWHERE

BEST THINKING IS FORGED THROUGH WRITING

A GENERAL WRITING PROCESS

DIALOGUE BRINGS STORY VIVIDLY TO MIND

WRITING CONTROL MUST REMAIN WITH WRITER

This student enjoys expressing herself through writing.

**WRITING GIVES STUDENTS
A VOICE TO BE HEARD**

Share Experiences. Tell your student about the saddest, most embarrassing, happiest or funniest experience you have had. Have him or her do the same, and then both of you write stories around them. Involve the student's sense of justice and fair play by asking for written comments on various human issues and concerns. Discrimination and prejudice in the school (or in the community or world at large) might be two such issues, and you might follow up by reading both current and past novels and plays that deal with them. Encourage all students to take stands on issues about which they feel strongly. Writing about such topics gives students a voice to be heard. It allows them to think through problems clearly, safely, as they experience a form of power over the world around them.

**STRONG EMOTIONS
POWERFUL WRITING
CATALYSTS**

Strongly felt emotions, from love to anger, are powerful catalysts for serious writing. When students see their feelings expressed on paper, it will be like seeing parts of themselves on the page. They will value writing only if they see it is a worthwhile and authentic means of self-expression.

New Endings

Write new endings to an exciting story. Stop reading before the climax, then both of you write a satisfying conclusion. Read each other's work. Ask your student to comment on your writing and then do the same for him or her. Finally, read the original ending from the text and discuss how it compares with both of yours.

WRITE FINAL SCENES FOR PLAYS

Write the final scene of a film: one that has a family split up, there are many. After students have gained prior experience of the script by playing the characters involved, ask them to write a final jury scene, awarding the child to one of the parents indicating the reason for their choice through the judge's dialogue.

Drama and Role-playing. This is an excellent medium to practice reading and writing skills. The interview is one form of drama. Interview your student, who takes on the identity of someone in a well known historical event, film, or novel. Use the "hot seat" format. For example, the tutor can interview the student as the Captain of the Titanic, one of the passengers, or an explorer who has just surfaced from the wreck on the ocean floor. The dialogue generated by this role-playing can be written as a play and then read before an audience, if the student wishes.

"HOT SEAT" INTERVIEW FORMAT

Modelling. Collaborate often when writing with your student. Teach writing by example. This type of modelling is a very effective method. The student may begin to internalize your methods and also become an independent writer who uses all the stages of writing on his or her way to a polished final draft.

COLLABORATION HELPS STUDENTS INTERNALIZE PROCESS

That's why writing on identical topics at the same time is a good idea. Edit each other's work by writing down positive comments about where to go next. Also consider co-authoring plays about issues that concern you. Themes can evolve from everyday experiences or news reports. Dramatize these plays by acting them out, or tape record polished final scripts for an invited audience of other tutors and students.

DRAMATIZE YOUR PLAYS

Add Variety. As your student develops ability, ensure he or she experiences a variety of writing modes. All writing stems from our own lives. Even fantasy formats such as "What if... I was a race car driver, a rock star, etc." are prompts for describing our likes and dislikes and help us develop our own voice. Encourage the student to use the paper as a canvas on which to "paint" favourite scenes with vivid, colourful description.

ALL WRITING FROM SELF

To develop expository (explanatory) writing, ask your student to write about topics you, the tutor, know nothing about, thereby teaching *you* through writing. When reading a student's initial drafts, ask questions

ALLOW YOUR STUDENT TO TEACH YOU

QUESTIONS WILL LEAD
TO CLARITY

which will lead to clarity. When teaching expository writing read models of subjects the student is interested in: "How To" books involving sports and other activities, for instance.

STUDENTS SHOULD READ
MODELS

Before students begin to write, also read various examples of the writing mode to be explored. John Parker's, *Writing Workshop*, has some excellent examples of student writing, as do many of James Moffat's texts. Mark Twain's description of Pap, Huck's father in *The Adventures of Huckleberry Finn*, is a fine descriptive model, as are the final paragraphs of F. Scott Fitzgerald's, *The Great Gatsby*. Advertisements from magazines are another good choice for modelling descriptive writing.

TRY PHOTO STIMULUS

When a student suffers a writing block, use photo stimulus. The student can discuss intriguing or puzzling photographs with you and then write about them. Often you can brainstorm topics and write key words and concepts on paper or on the board in point form.

Drafts and Editing. Don't correct the spelling of beginning writer's drafts, unless you're asked. Allow the student to circle words he or she thinks may not be spelled correctly. In this fashion, your students will learn the responsibility of editing their writing. To encourage the drafting process, ask local professional writers (there are many people who write in any community) to visit and show students their successive drafts and the final, published products. When students see that "real" writers create a number of drafts, they will view the process as necessary exploration.

INVITE WRITERS FROM
YOUR COMMUNITY TO
CLASS

Often, students don't want to revise simply because they don't know they can get to excellence by successive drafts, leading to polished work. Show them a number of your drafts or copies.

Letters. To gain an audience, your teacher may be able to set up a letter network with grade two or grade three students. When your students write to these primary children, they will be aware of an audience receiving their letters and will attempt to do their best. The teachers can act as postmen when the children write back. Letter writing of this kind may be the first step towards a visit by your students who can act as teachers of reading and writing to primary children. This format has worked very well in my classes.

WRITE AND THEN VISIT
PRIMARY CHILDREN

The Experience Story. If none of these techniques seems to inspire students who appear traumatized about writing, use the experience story described in Chapter 4 for initial assignments. At first, this kind of story is printed for your student to read, but later proceed to write it in your best hand so the student can copy it. You or the school's Practice Typing Office can type these stories. At the end of the year, students using this format will have the equivalent of a published novel all about themselves.

USE EXPERIENCE STORY
FOR WRITING

In a positive environment even the most reluctant student will write.

The experience story has many uses. One particularly successful instance was with a deaf student who disdained reading the books in the Reading Room, because she didn't understand many of the concepts. On the other hand, we noticed how dramatically she was using sign language to tell her own stories. The Reading Tutor asked her to tell her own experience story in sign while she copied it down word for word.

Luckily, the day before the girl had had a very significant experience. In this world of silence, one of her best friends at the time was her cat. The student described how she wore big floppy sweaters and how her cat would crawl up in her sweater for an afternoon doze. That day, when she awoke, she found two kittens in her sweater! Telling her story in sign language, she was very excited as you can well imagine! Because the incident was so vivid in her memory, she read it back to the tutor with relative ease. She had no problem whatever with syntax, semantics or the concepts, because they were all her own. The tutor, standing behind her student, following silently as she read orally, understood her speech for

SYNTAX, SEMANTICS AND CONCEPTS ARE THE STUDENT'S

CONFIDENT STUDENTS
WILL WRITE ON THEIR OWN

the first time. Her tutor continued to use this format every day. Consequently, this student made significant gains in reading, writing and oral language. Once students have acquired confidence and an awareness of writing through the experience story mode, they will begin to write on their own. Encourage them to do this as soon as they are ready.

THE RELUCTANT WRITER

AT FIRST, MODEL WRITING

To get your students started, you need to provide a positive writing environment through modelling writing and reading until they feel secure and confident enough to write. Let them collaborate on your writing. However, be prepared for the reluctant student. One very good tutor was upset and blamed herself because, although her student was learning to read, he refused to write for some time during the first semester. He wasn't pushed, and when he did begin to write, he did so with enjoyment. He had never written before, and this was a tremendous accomplishment for him and for his tutor.

MANY POOR READERS
HAVE EXCELLENT
MEMORIES

USE TELEVISION TO
ADVANTAGE

While personal experience stories are always a fine medium for writing, description by the student of favourite films or television shows has great potential for writing. In fact, because students who don't read well must constantly commit information to memory, they often have developed the ability to remember in detail. Frequently, a tutor will be offered almost all the incidents of a film by his or her student rather than a basic plot outline. As a result, all kinds of writing can be generated with the help of the good old television.

THE WORD PROCESSOR

WORD PROCESSOR
WRITING LOOKS
PROFESSIONAL

Most students are very positive about using a word processor. The reason is obvious: products look better, more professional, and many word processors make spelling and editing easy. These benefits will please your student every bit as much as they do anyone else. If you have word processors in your school, certainly use them in conjunction with teaching your student to write. The biggest plus, of course, is the editing capability. Words and lines can be changed and rearranged with great ease. At first, you might only be involved in typing the final drafts for your student's folder. As soon as possible, act as an editor, write with your student, producing polished efforts for the student's writing file, which demonstrate extensive writing process.

USE WORD PROCESSOR
RIGHT AWAY IF STUDENT
WISHES

Some students may want to use the "word pros" right away. That's great. Let them do so! After all, an objective for all tutors is to have their student take the initiative and produce their "own stuff" on the word processor.

COLLABORATIONS

ALLOW STUDENT TO MAKE EDITING SUGGESTIONS ABOUT YOUR WRITING

At the end of the year, a good writing activity is one in which both tutor and students collaborate to write an anthology of stories and articles for publication. Each makes his or her contributions, either independently or collectively, including the illustrations, advertisements, editing and assembling. Because it is a joint project, here is a chance for your student to read your writing and make positive suggestions about it. If you treat students as equals, you will find that you've given them considerable self-esteem and confidence. The finished products can be delivered to the family of schools from which your student came.

CURSIVE WRITING

WRITING IS MORE RAPID THAN PRINTING

Sometimes, you'll find that the students you work with avoid writing in favour of printing, but their printing may be very poor, as shown in Appendix C. This is often due to bad habits or underdeveloped hand-eye co-ordination. Cursive writing ability is a necessary skill in a writing world, a social value upon which your student may be judged as an adult. If students only print, and sloppily, opinions about them may be negative. Poor printing may be a difficult habit to break, and it is often far easier to teach them writing instead. Also, writing is much faster than printing, because the student does not have to lift the pen from the paper, as writing flows. Neat writing will instill a sense of pride in achievement and definitely aid in the entire writing process.

CORRECTING — RED INK OUT THE WINDOW

DO NOT DEFACE WRITING

NO NEED FOR "HACK" MARKS

DON'T USE ABSOLUTE STANDARDS

Red ink for corrections, or any other colour for that matter, should not be used when working with your student's drafts. Red ink may be responsible for your student feeling so discouraged in the past. A student hates nothing more than seemingly vicious or insulting hack marks all over his or her writing. In actuality, there is no practical reason for this type of correction, for you are there at your student's side every minute of the writing period to assist in all aspects of drafts and editing. The result you are seeking is a student who is free from the fear of low marks and multitudes of corrections and who enjoys writing without the fear of censure.

You should, however, offer at least two types of comments in writing on any draft: a positive specific statement and one asking a leading question. Never hold your student to an abstract writing standard,

Students learn to write by writing.

because such an absolute will only create a greater reluctance to write. Instead help your student on to the next level of accomplishment.

There are alternatives to marking or grading. A polished piece of student work can simply be read with interest and admiration. With the author's permission, it might be read to other tutors and even the whole class. Teachers are frequently quite positive about such initiatives. You might even want to tape or dramatize a story before placing it in the student's personal file. Attention from appreciative audiences other than the Reading Tutor creates an atmosphere of celebration, of pleasure for the writer.

APPRECIATIVE AUDIENCES CREATE A CELEBRATION OF WRITING

If the mark for your student is not based only on improvement, but on the number of writing assignments submitted, then give him or her 100 perfect marks at the beginning of the term. Starting a student out at 100% usually means that he or she will be reluctant to drop down by missing assignments, particularly if an A has always been out of reach.

START WITH 100%

SUCCESS STORIES — PROMOTE THEM!

STUDENTS WILL WANT TO
WRITE AT LENGTH IF THEY
FEEL SUCCESSFUL

One student assigned to a tutor had entered secondary school reading below a grade two level and with only basic printing skills. At first, producing a third of a page of printing was a difficult task. At the end of the semester, this student had accumulated seventy-five pages of work in his writing folder. He became very enthused about writing because many of his polished drafts were read to assembled tutors and students and drew considerable applause. Because of his diligence and consistent effort, he moved from printing to writing and, indeed, to writing in a relatively fine manner (See Appendix C).

This success story points out quite forcefully that students learn writing by constantly writing, not by memorizing rules of grammar or spelling. Obviously, fluency in oral language is not gained through drill but through conversing with others, modelling speech patterns, and inferring word meanings as a result.

SOME CONCLUSIONS

SHARE YOUR OWN
STRATEGIES AT MEETINGS

While this chapter has been a general guide on the teaching of writing, remember you are a creative, imaginative, free-thinking individual. No doubt, you can develop unique strategies of your own to enhance your student's opportunity to enjoy and improve his or her writing. Don't forget to share with your tutor peer group and supervising teacher any of your own strategies for teaching reading and writing during weekly brainstorming sessions.

Finally, you may find this selected list of comments useful. They come from tutors whose students were in different stages of development.

APPROACH DEPENDS ON
WRITER'S DEVELOPMENT

- Creative narrative: he tells a story, but I must ask lots of questions.

- "The Weekend" is a good writing topic.

- Heavy dialogue leads to good writing.

- Must help my student with spelling as she writes.

- My student wants no help with anything until the second draft. I think he wants to surprise me with his story.

- Talk about what he knows/what he likes.

- Read a book or an article from a magazine, then write.

- My student writes about his most frightening experience, his saddest memory, his happiest, the funniest-thing essay.

Favourite desserts can be a writing topic!

• Talk, then point form, then write, seems to work well for us.

• She likes to write about herself: "A Day in the Life of …."

• He is interested in a lot of things, but I must dig for them.

• Watch facial expression: you don't have to ask when it's time to quit and go on to other things.

THERE IS A MULTITUDE OF APPROACHES

• Use oral language written down.

• He will write, if I promise to type his final draft. I'm getting good at typing.

• My student will only write in isolation because of embarrassment.

• I help her with drafts only when she asks. She knows when she needs help.

• He likes to write his opinion about things. I don't disagree, and I help him only when he asks. (At some point a little constructive disagreement helps to dislodge more hidden ideas.)

- My student won't write unless I help him all the way.

- Conversation always makes some writing topic come up.

- Favourite desserts are my student's favourite writing topic!

- When writing, my student likes to imagine he is a famous boxer or wrestler.

BE INNOVATIVE

- We write and mail fan letters to movie stars—creative narrative's the best.

- Topics! a party, a dream—just talk, talk, talk.

- I read his rough draft aloud. When he notices mistakes, I correct them.

- I let her read her rough draft out loud. When she can't make it out, we make corrections.

ALLOW YOUR STUDENT
TO TEACH WRITING

- We write to grade two students. We edit our work with care. They write back. We visit and teach reading. My student sees himself as a reading teacher!

- I always praise the final draft. It always deserves it.

- My student likes to draw a picture first and then write about it.

- We went to the zoo on Saturday; he wrote about the animals for two weeks.

DEVELOP YOUR OWN KEY
TO STUDENT'S WRITING

- We write down song lyrics. She loves music. We listen to records and pick up all the words.

- He hates writing but doesn't mind talking into the tape recorder and then writing it down.

- New endings for stories and movies.

- I must draw him out: mirror his experiences in my own life.

- Ask her opinion.

- She writes about her family.

- We write letters to magazines trying to win contests. There are a million contests!

CHAPTER 6

Tutoring English as a Second Language and English Skills Development

OFTEN, **THE STUDENTS** you encounter come from other countries and have varied linguistic and cultural backgrounds. Their educations may be very different from yours.

STUDENTS MAY HAVE
DIFFERENT REQUIREMENTS

These students *may* require English as a Second Language (ESL). Or, if there have been gaps in their education, they may need assistance with English Skills Development (ESD). Because there are so many variables in culture, language and education, these students need your support to acquire more than basic language skills. They require the opportunity to develop feelings of self-worth, personal acceptance and academic success to achieve their potential as individuals.

RECEPTION

OFTEN A DIFFICULT
ADJUSTMENT

Remember, first impressions are lasting! By the time you meet the students, they will already have a timetable and have met many people. This doesn't mean they will know their way around or feel comfortable. If you will be working with someone who has been in the country for several years, be prepared for feelings of inadequacy or frustration.

These may only indicate that the student has not yet been successful in making the difficult adjustments necessary to succeed in our system. You can make the difference! You can provide the necessary support in a sensitive and responsive relationship.

KNOW HOW TO SUPPORT
YOUR STUDENT

Providing Support. You can give it in a variety of ways. Some students may be taking ESL courses for credit, in sections of other subject areas geared to ESL students' requirements, in regular classes with some modifications for them, or in classes where no modifications are provided. It is essential for you to know how much support your student is receiving so you can plan effectively.

HELP YOUR STUDENT
ADJUST

Your Objective. Give ESL or ESD students the opportunity to become better in English so they can be successful in the regular school program. Your aim is to help them adjust to their new environment. It is

Tutor motivates her student to interact with others

OBJECTIVES BASED ON
STUDENT'S NEEDS

up to you to provide experiences that are varied, relevant and rich. Only then can you motivate your student to communicate, to interact with others and become familiar with the this country's cultural mosaic. On a one-to-one level, specific objectives must be based on the needs of your student.

ORIENTATION

ORIENTATION FIRST

Bear in mind that students may arrive at any time during the school year. No matter when your student arrives, he or she will initially require some degree of orientation. On the first day, help him or her become acquainted with the new environment. During the first week, help your student become oriented by assistance with the following:

1. a walk around the school to locate classrooms, cafeteria, office, resource centre, etc.

2. practice using a combination lock

3. learn daily routines (schedule, rules, code of behaviour, school calendar, lunch procedures, etc.)

4. become familiar with school personnel and subjects taught

5. practice appropriate language for ordering in the cafeteria and asking for assistance

6. talk about the differences between this school system and the one from which he or she came.

SOCIO-CULTURAL FACTORS

VALUES ARE BASED ON CULTURE AND LIFE EXPERIENCES.

Your student's life experiences will differ from yours; so will socio-cultural background. The day to day things you take for granted may be completely unknown. In some cultures, for example, it is impolite to look an adult in the eye. To us, avoiding eye contact might indicate shyness, evasiveness or even impolite behaviour. In some other cultures, males have a higher status than females, so a girl's education may not be equally valued. If you are in doubt in a particular situation, don't hesitate to discuss it with your student or your teacher. Remember, values are based on culture and life experience. Use the opportunity to expand knowledge—yours and your student's.

PLAN ACTIVITIES THAT BUILD LANGUAGE EXPERIENCES.

PLAN ACTIVITIES THAT BUILD LANGUAGE EXPERIENCES.

The Experience Base. Language must be developed from a student's own experience if you are to strengthen basic communication skills. The student must be able to see language as a valuable tool for everyday purposes. Plan activities that build the experiences he or she will need to become an active participant in the new environment. As an added advantage, these experiences will become subjects about which to write. Simple things like the grocery store, bus system or the movie theatre can be new and exciting!

DEVELOPING LANGUAGE

Acquiring a second language is much like learning a first language, but these are important differences. With young children, language progresses from cooing and babbling, to first words, to two connected words, and then rapidly expands. Syntax and semantics steadily develop. Some of these skills are not fully acquired until the age of ten or twelve. Second language *acquisition* is much like learning a mother tongue. *Language learning,* on the other hand, refers to direct instruction: being taught about the language (grammar).

USE LANGUAGE IN
PRACTICAL AND
MEANINGFUL WAYS.

When learning a second language, success has a lot to do with the crucial factors of the learning situation, amount of exposure to the language, motivation and the learner's comfort level. Therefore, it is extremely important for you to ensure your student has opportunities to use language in practical and meaningful ways in real life situations. Research and experience have shown that learning isolated vocabulary and conjugating verbs do not enable a learner to function in a second language. In fact, you may have already discovered this in your own attempts to learn a second language. For these reasons, you should use a "whole language" approach with your ESL and ESL students. Don't fragment language instruction; teach it as a complete, real life tool.

DON'T FRAGMENT
LANGUAGE—TEACH
IT AS A "WHOLE".

Language differences.   Learning to speak a second language requires the use of different sounds, words, sentence structures and even orthography (writing). There may or may not be counterparts for any of these in a student's first language. Those that are similar will come easily; those that aren't will be more difficult to acquire. French speakers, for instance, often have difficulty with the "th" sound (as in "thank"). English speakers frequently have difficulty with the guttural sounds in German. Listen carefully to your student. You may notice that he or she consistently uses one sound in place of another. Concentrate on these areas.

LANGUAGES MAY HAVE
SIMILARITIES AND
DIFFERENCES.

The goal.   Never lose sight of your primary goal. You are assisting your student to learn English so he or she can fully participate in school activities and in the community. The purpose is to enhance participation in all subject areas, either to continue on to post-secondary education or to find appropriate employment. Always remember that the objectives you set must be based on the student's individual needs.

THE GOAL IS TO
PARTICIPATE IN THE
SCHOOL AND
COMMUNITY.

VARIABLES

There are several other non-linguistic factors that affect second language acquisition.

Age.   Young children *appear* to acquire a second language very quickly. Adolescents may seem reluctant to speak another language for fear of appearing inadequate. Adults bring a lot of first language ability with them and are eager to transfer knowledge and skill. However, at any age there may be a "silent period" that may last from a few days to a few months. Don't panic! This is common.

EXPECT A "SILENT" PERIOD.

The student has high academic skills in her first language and made rapid progress

Although you would like your student to progress as quickly as possible, it is important to know that it takes approximately five to seven years for ESL students to reach the level of their peers. They may appear to be doing well orally, but it still takes about two years to master everyday language.

Educational background. The success your student has in the school program will be closely tied to the previous system and its similarities to ours. Another major factor is literacy. Is your student literate in his or her mother tongue? If so, then a transfer of skills will assist both you and your student. If not, you will have to begin filling in the gaps.

LITERACY IN THE FIRST LANGUAGE ENABLES A STUDENT TO TRANSFER SKILLS.

Self image. Perhaps the most important variable in language acquisition is your student's self image. Is culture shock still a problem? Is motivation weak? That is, has he or she chosen to learn English, or has he or she been forced? Anxiety, homesickness, fear of rejection and self consciousness are some of the most crippling feelings a student may experience. In planning your lessons, always include objectives in

SELF IMAGE MAY BE THE MOST IMPORTANT VARIABLE.

these three areas: attitudes, skills and knowledge. With the right approach, you can both accomplish almost anything.

ESL STRATEGIES

When selecting listening, speaking, reading and writing strategies, let your student's needs and abilities dictate your choices. Before choosing, though, you should know:

1. some students will require a long period of listening before they are comfortable enough to speak

2. fluency is more important than grammatical accuracy

3. in conversation, only errors that interfere with meaning should be corrected (negative miscues)

4. all types of interaction are vital to language acquisition

5. small group activities invite participation

6. tutor dominated discussions are not effective in oral language development

7. students literate in their first language will readily transfer knowledge

8. writing should begin as a collaborate effort with the tutor.

Reading assignments should be related to prior experience. Discuss or view a film to prepare the student for both the language and the concepts that will be presented. Writing should centre on the student's interests and experiences and be aimed at skill development. The strategies that follow are listed by individual language skills. However, remember that class material is presented in a holistic manner.

Listening.   Give your student the opportunity to listen to stories, respond to such requests as "stand up" or "raise your hand," draw a picture according to a set of instructions, listen to a recorded interview and fill out information about it on a prepared form.

Speaking.   Help your student learn "survival language" such as his or her name, address, and typical greetings. Ask activities to be named as they are mimed by other students (eating, painting, writing). Practice short dialogues useful in specific situations inside and outside class. Role-play to learn the appropriate language and non-verbal behaviour required when speaking to the principal, peers, cafeteria staff, bus drivers, and staff in a movie theatre. Explore how to introduce a new classmate and how to interact with visitors to class. Learn how to work with other students on collaborative or interactive computer programs.

WHEN SPEAKING, CORRECT ONLY ERRORS THAT INTERFERE WITH MEANING.

PREPARE YOUR STUDENT FOR THE LANGUAGE AND THE CONCEPTS.

PRACTICE USEFUL LANGUAGE AND APPROPRIATE NON-VERBAL BEHAVIOUR.

DEVELOP LANGUAGE
EXPERIENCE STORES.

READ A VARIETY OF
MATERIALS.

Reading.   Have your student participate in developing language experience stories. Practice sequential thought by assembling comics, recipes or instructions. Ask for a summary of a passage. Be sure to have your student read a variety of materials: advertisements, newspapers, menus, maps, signs, forms, short stories, examinations and so on. Once an appropriate literary passage has been read, ask for a response.

Writing.   Ask your student to keep a personal journal. Assist in writing letters to fellow students, teachers or people at other schools. Help him or her use computer word processing programs to develop polished pieces. Keep a writing folder to demonstrate development. Use the writing process technique described in Chapter 5.

ESD Strategies

PROVIDE A SUPPORTIVE
ENVIRONMENT.

When working with a student who has limited or no formal education, you will have to provide opportunities to develop basic literacy. Remember to begin with the student's own experiences. These, combined with varied and rich activities, will help to foster a positive attitude toward language and literacy. A student trying to close a gap in his or her educational background will be sensitive. When selecting strategies, provide a supportive environment that encourages risk-taking.

Speaking and listening.   Invite a variety of speakers to address the class so you student can listen. Encourage participation in role-playing. Have your student interview a number of people and report to the class.

USE APPROPRIATE
PICTURE DICTIONARIES.

Reading.   At first, develop basic reading skills by having your student match letters of the alphabet with samples, including capital and lower case letters. Ask him or her to read such personal information as name, address and telephone number. Filling in the blanks in a language experience story, putting the sentences in sequence, and compiling a personal word list are all useful strategies. Using appropriate picture dictionaries can also be helpful. Be sure to read a variety of materials using the techniques from the chapters on teaching reading. Finally, encourage your student to keep a reading log.

PRACTICE WRITING
CONVENTIONS IN
CONTEXT.

Writing.   Learning correct letter formation and writing conventions (left to right, top to bottom of page) are essential strategies. Practice upper and lower case printing and cursive script, then move on to combining letters into words. Learn capitalization and punctuation in the context of the writing process. Fill out application forms. Use a word processing program to develop polished writing. Keep a journal and a writing folder.

Social integration is very important

SHARE YOUR STRATEGIES
WITH OTHER TUTORS.

These are just a few suggestions to use with ESL and ESD students. For an ESD student, review Chapter 7. No doubt, you will come up with many more strategies on your own Be sure to share them with other tutors at your weekly meetings. Then you will all end up with an extensive portfolio of useful ideas.

INTEGRATION

YOUR STUDENT MUST FEEL
COMFORTABLE IN THE
SCHOOL AND COMMUNITY.

Integration for your student is a two-fold process. First, he or she must fit in and be able to succeed in subject areas. Second, and more important, is the ability to fit into the school and neighbourhood communities. There is little point in working with your student on a geography assignment when he or she is unsure of the proximity of home to the school or even where the washrooms are.

Social integration is often the most difficulty to address, yet it must precede academic integration. Many ESL and ESD students readily see

SOCIAL ACTIVITIES PRESENT AN OPPORTUNITY TO PRACTICE LANGUAGE SKILLS.

the value of academic pursuits but don't accept that joining a club or sports team will help them get ahead. Explain to your student that participating in social activities presents a real opportunity to practice and increase language abilities in real life situations.

School club and team participation will help your student speak like his or her peers, an added and desirable benefit. Success with such school activities also leads to social integration in the larger community, because with some support your student will be more apt to join similar groups in the community. All these opportunities offer the student the ability to become an active, contributing member of the community. This is our ultimate goal.

SOCIAL INTEGRATION IS OUR ULTIMATE GOAL.

Academic integration, on the other hand, involves both language and concepts. Your student has studied certain subjects before coming to this country. The concepts will be there, but the related vocabulary won't. Alternately, your student may have no previous experience in a subject. Therefore, both new concepts and new vocabulary will have to be acquired simultaneously—a much more difficult endeavour.

IT IS MORE DIFFICULT TO ACQUIRE NEW CONCEPTS AND LANGUAGE SIMULTANEOUSLY.

Imagine yourself learning multiplication in Russian. You already have the concepts, so you must concentrate on the vocabulary. Now imagine yourself in a Russian class on fibre-optic technology. Chances are you have neither the concepts nor the vocabulary. Which situation would your prefer?

Understandably, ESL and ESD students learning both the concepts and the language require assistance that is focused in two very specific ways:

English for Academic Purposes (EAP).   In an academic setting, we often take much for granted: how assignments are to be handed in, writing styles, bibliographies, tables, charts, graphs and so on. The focus here is to assist with these conventions.

ASSIST YOUR STUDENT WITH EXPECTATIONS FOR ASSIGNMENTS.

English for Specific Purposes (ESP).   In this focus, the tutor assists with language in specific disciplines such as technological studies, English necessary for particular co-op placements, after-school jobs and the like.

Successful integration depends on everyone's co-operation. During this difficult time it is important to recognize your student's need to use his or her first language in certain circumstances. If you had the advantage of a translator during the Russian lecture on fibre-optic technology, the translation would have acted as a bridge between concept and language. Probably, your learning would have accelerated. Be careful with your student, though. Don't use translation as a crutch. Find the fine line between dependency and assistance.

USE TRANSLATION AS A BRIDGE BETWEEN CONCEPT AND LANGUAGE.

Through all of this bear in mind that ESL and ESD students often have a language repertoire. They already speak one language, perhaps two or more, before meeting you. English is simply another language

ENGLISH IS BEING ADDED TO YOUR STUDENT'S LANGUAGE REPERTOIRE.

in their repertoire; it does not replace their mother tongue. Be careful to show respect for your student's language and culture. This, in turn, will indicate your respect for that individual.

EVALUATIONS

EVALUATION MUST BE ENCOURAGING.

The evaluation of a student's growth in language learning must be continuously encouraging. Adjust your expectations to the length of time your student has been in the country, previous educational experiences and the amount of cultural adjustment required.

ADJUST YOUR EXPECTATIONS.

TAKE ORAL SAMPLES USING A TAPE RECORDER.

Some students will become quite frustrated if they think they are not progressing fast enough. You may find it helpful to take oral samples using a tape recorder every four weeks. Then you can let them hear what they sounded like a month or ever four months earlier.

FOCUS ON WHERE YOUR STUDENT IS NOW.

Beyond this technique, the information on evaluation covered in Chapter 12 also applies to ESL and ESD students. Your student must be familiar with this criteria as well. For your part, you should focus on where your student is now compared to where he or she began.

HOW HAS THE PROGRAM INFLUENCED STUDENT PERFORMANCE?

When you evaluate your program for your student, the focus is on ways in which it might have influenced student performance. Program evaluation considers the objectives, content, teaching strategies, material and student progress by answering the following questions:

Objectives.   Were the objectives based on your student's needs? Did the course help the student develop, become confident, and maintain a sense of self-worth?

ENCOURAGE STUDENTS TO SHARE ASPECTS OF THEIR CULTURE.

Content.   Did the units studied help the student understand and be more aware of the new environment? To what extent was the difficulty of the material adjusted to suit the needs and backgrounds of the student? What were some of the most and least productive activities? Were the choice and sequence of topics appropriate? To foster understanding, were students encouraged to share aspects of their cultures?

MAXIMIZE INTERACTION.

Strategies.   To what degree were your methods of instruction varied to match the needs and background of the student? Did the classroom environment encourage maximum student participation and interaction? Did activities encourage your student to participate, initially as an observer, and later more actively?

Materials.   Were materials that reflected the student's culture available? Was a variety of non-print materials available?

ACCURATE RECORDS?

Progress. Were accurate records kept of the student's work and participation throughout the course? Use benchmarks or standards to help you determine your student's progress.

NEW BEGINNINGS

The information contained in this chapter is meant as an introduction to the world of ESL and ESD. The experiences you have with your student will be the true learning opportunity for both of you.

Immigration implies both new beginnings and responsibilities. As a person new to the country, many adjustments must be made while learning a new language and developing skills. By participating in the Reading Tutor Program, you have shown a desire to make a difference in your student's life and his or her future in this country.

Just as an immigrant or refugee has made a commitment to a new life here, we, as the host country, have also accepted the responsibility to assist each one to become a valuable, contributing member of our community. In a very personal way, you are the first step in this process. I am sure you will find working with ESL and ESD students a unique and rewarding experience.

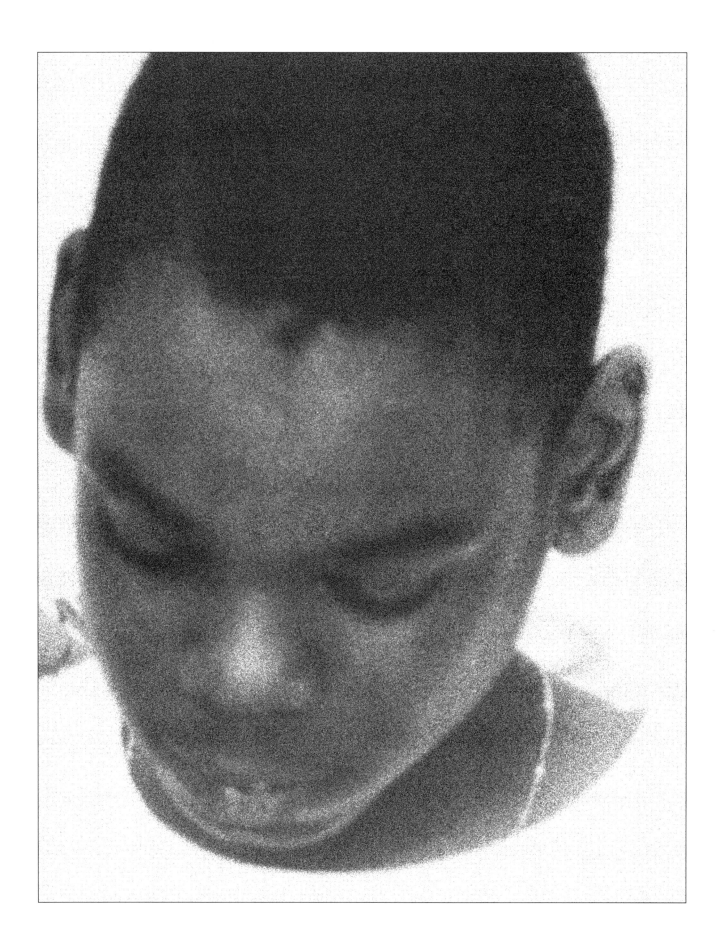

CHAPTER 7

Reading and Writing for Elementary School Children

To A Large Extent much of what you have already learned in previous chapters applies to teaching reading and writing to anyone, including young children. However, when tutoring at the elementary level you should know about some specific methods, ways of developing prior experience, reading materials and stages of reading.

Personal, first hand experience is even more important to children in the elementary grades. As you know from Chapter 2, the act of reading depends to a large extent on the personal connections we make with the reading material. The younger the child, the more tenuous are these links to "non-visual information." It is important for you, the Reading Tutor, to firm up and reinforce these connections between the child's inner world and what will be read. This is best done as a pre-reading experience that may consist of a walk outside if you're reading about the weather, cooking porridge if you're reading about Goldilocks or dressing up as a witch for a Halloween story.

Such a preparatory strategy allows the child to recall and consolidate the pre-reading experience, and it gives you a chance to introduce vocabulary in the context of the real world. When the child's porridge is "too hot," "too cold" or "just right," predicting the sequence in Goldilocks becomes much easier. When a pre-reading session is not convenient, the next best thing is a discussion centred around the book's illustrations before actual reading begins.

Like *Goldilocks*, many children's books are beautifully illustrated, and they can be used to make books a positive part of the rich fantasy land of imagination that little people often visit and love so well. These illustrations are a perfect vehicle to build a young reader's prior experience of any story. In many primary and junior story books, the illustrations are either above, below or to the left of the print. Most often, they are a visual description or replication of the words.

An actual lesson given to a grade three boy may help you begin to understand how illustrations can be used to teach reading. The title was *Meg at Sea*, by Helen Nicoll and Jan Pienkowski. The initial illustration shows a witch, her cat and owl at the beach. The printed story reads: "Meg, Mog and Owl went to the seaside." The essence of the

CONCRETE EXPERIENCES IMPORTANT TO YOUNG STUDENTS

VISIT RICH FANTASY WORLD

USE ILLUSTRATIONS TO BUILD PRIOR EXPERIENCE

The tutor enhances a student's ability to predict by having her tell the story first.

written story is captured in each of the illustrations, which is true of most beginning reader's books.

Often, elementary school children who don't read or who are just beginning will be far more intrigued by the illustrations than the words on the page. Therefore, you should always explore the drawings on each page before initiating reading. In your conversation, incorporate the words about to be read as you ask questions about the illustration. This will help the child predict from context.

With *Meg at Sea*, the tutor invited the child to tell the story using only the illustration. The boy said, "An old witch, a cat and a big bird are at the beach." The tutor responded, "Yes, that's right, doesn't it look like fun?" Then she went on to ask her student, "What kind of bird is that in the picture?" The boy didn't know, so the tutor revealed it was Owl, and the witch's name was Meg, and the cat's Mog. She continued, "Yes, they went to the beach; when it's beside the ocean, it's called a seaside."

At this point, the tutor should be ready to read the first page of the story to the student; alternatively, read it together or have the student

INCORPORATE WORDS TO BE READ

EXPLORE DRAWINGS IN THE BOOK TO BE READ

POINT AT IMAGE OF KEY WORDS

ASK FACTUAL AND HIGHER LEVEL THINKING SKILL QUESTIONS

IMBUE STORIES WITH MAGIC AND FUN

BEGINNING READERS WILL APPROXIMATE MEANING

DETAILED DISCUSSIONS ELICIT A GREATER CHANCE OF ACCURATE PREDICTION

read it. The choice depends on the student's stage of development. In this case, the tutor had the child read it by himself, but with her active assistance. As he read, she pointed at the illustration when he encountered key words. For instance, she pointed to Owl when the word was about to be read, and so on.

Follow this method when building prior experience of a story. Say, "What do you think this book is about?" Ask questions that not only involve factual information gained from the illustration, but also inferential, evaluative and hypothetical questions as part of your natural discussion of the story. Make this part of your method for all elementary students: pre-reading, emergent or independent. This technique will not only develop your student's ability to predict meaning and words (the strongest reading strategy), but it will imbue stories with magic and pure fun. It is vital that your student develops a positive attitude toward reading, and where possible makes a personal connection with some of a story's elements. Ask: "Have you ever done this?" "Have you ever seen one of these?" "Have you ever pretended to be...?"

A student who is aware that print carries meaning, and one who doesn't yet make the connection, may "read" stories in different ways. In both cases, if you have used effective prior experience strategies, your student will often approximate the meaning and may, in fact, use some of the words on the page in his or her telling of the story. This a positive step, because it allows him or her to make connections between the words and illustrations as the story's meaning is extracted, even though the exact words have not been repeated. Remember our earlier discussion about the importance of not correcting **positive miscues.** With elementary school children or with any reader, precise word replication is not desirable because it indicates over attention to the print, the surface structure of reading.

Frequently, students in the very early stages of reading may construct the story based entirely on their recollection of what they have heard and gained from viewing and discussing the pictures. Your task is to sense the readiness of the student to pay more attention to the print. This may require you to read the story and make references to particular words: "This word is a really long one; it means...." For small groups, large format "big books" are also an effective strategy.

The more detailed your discussion of the illustrations with young readers, the greater will be their chance of predicting the printed words and correct meanings of stories. The more often they see themselves as right in reading, the more positive they will become about their involvement with books. This is the Reading Tutor's major task with elementary school children.

In the sentence, "On Sunday morning we go to *church*," many children will predict the final word accurately. Cover it abruptly as a method to encourage your student to use prediction in favour of

Students are proud of reading well for their tutors.

HELP STUDENTS DEVELOP
A PREFERENCE FOR
PREDICTION

word replication. Do this often, and your student should begin to prefer prediction to "sounding out" as a reading method. With hesitant readers, this strategy can become a game. Read to your student and stop at predictable words. The student fills in the word, and then you continue reading. Make it explicit that the student can know the word without attending to any surface structure. After a successful response, say "Terrific! How did you know that?" Reinforce the process by saying, "Isn't it amazing how we can know what comes next without even seeing the word."

Hypothetically, if a picture in a child's book depicts a caterpillar on a branch, make sure either you or your student voices the words when extracting the story from its illustration. When reading the text, your student may then be able to predict both "caterpillar" and "branch" from their initial consonants. Children who do so will take great pride in reading such "big" words and view themselves as very good readers. Reinforce success with statements like, "You must be proud of yourself," or simply, "You are a good reader."

SMALL STUDENTS WILL BE
PROUD OF READING "BIG"
WORDS

USE BOOKS WITH BUILT-IN PREDICTION

Many of the best books for young children are highly predictable. A number of fine authors incorporate repetitive words or phrases throughout the stories they write. Robert Munsch, a popular author of young children's books, does this exceedingly well. In one of his stories, *Thomas's Snow Suit*, Thomas repeatedly says "No" to requests to put on his snow suit. Fledgling readers, as they follow along, will begin to realize when Thomas is about to say, "Nnnno!!" and will shyly repeat the word under their breaths as it arrives in context. With more confidence, gained from the pleasure of being right, they may begin to repeat the predictable words aloud as you read the story to them.

CHILDREN CAN BECOME INSTANT READERS

Other books incorporate direct prediction. In "What Comes Next" books, for example, a page (with appropriate illustration) may have the printed words: "Here is a cloud. What comes next?" The next page reads, "Rain comes next," and so on. Using such carefully crafted books, children not only can become instant readers, but will learn sequence skills as well. Guided by your clever and subtle prompting, they will learn that predicting is not only the strongest reading strategy, but the one that is the easiest and the most fun to use. Of course, to predict well your students constantly must attend to the meaning from which the pleasure of reading is derived.

ALLOW STUDENTS TO DRAW, THEN WRITE

"PUBLISH" STUDENT WRITING

Don't forget to use the experience story format with your students. Allow them to draw a picture then tell you a brief story about it. Take down their words exactly as they say them. Have them read the story back immediately. If they print or write these stories, you can go on to "publish" them by typing the story beneath their drawing. If you want to laminate their stories and bind them together, they will have produced books which may be placed in a school's library. No doubt they will be excited and proud to be "published authors" when they are "knee high to a grasshopper!"

EMERGENT READERS

TEACH EMERGENT READERS THE FUN, PLEASURE AND EXCITEMENT OF READING

USE "ONCE UPON A TIME"

Your students may not read at all or even understand the relationship of the stories to the printed words. These students are at an early pre-reading developmental stage and are categorized as Emergent Readers. The most important lesson they can learn from you is the fun, pleasure and excitement of reading. Read appropriate books with them that you think are terrific, ones that will stimulate great interest and affect them emotionally. Have fun by entering the world of story telling with them. Try poetry and rhyme. Use that opening line spoken down the centuries by us all, "Once upon a time…." Allow them to tell you stories. Similarly, tell them stories that you loved when you were little and any of your current favourites.

A student enjoys the fantasy world of books.

HELP STUDENTS TO
VALUE BOOKS

Most children at the Emergent Reader level will have experienced part of this pre-reading stage before they arrive in school. This is the level at which children learn to bond to and value books. Positive attitudes such as these are developed when parents tell stories or read to their children. Furthermore, such activities develop interest, excitement and a closeness to the parent and a feeling of being wanted which can be internalized and transformed into a love of books. This can be fostered by such subtle gestures as the way in which you handle, store and care for books. When working with young children, what you do is as important as what you say.

USE "NO WORD" BOOKS

For students at this developmental stage, you may want to use "no word books" that tell the story by a series of drawings only. Many of these books run to twenty or more pages. They can form a direct entry into the fantasy or make believe world of stories. Have your students tell the story from beginning to end using the graphic clues in the illustrations as you help them learn to predict meaning without relying on phonics. This habit will enhance their reading ability when confronting printed words later on.

READ TO YOUR STUDENTS FREQUENTLY

At this stage, dramatization of familiar stories can build the bridge between books and the inner experience of a story. Remember, it is of primary importance that you read to your student frequently and employ all modes of communication to convey the stories being read. Giving children an opportunity to respond, by drawing, painting or dramatizing allows them to connect their personal understanding to the stories they hear.

PRINT AWARENESS

STUDENTS BEGIN TO DEVELOP AN AWARENESS OF THE FUNCTION OF PRINT

The next stage of reading development is Print Awareness. Children at this level become aware that the words they "read" correspond to those printed on the page, that print is read from left to right, and that print consists of letters and words. At first, these children should be encouraged to participate in the story actively by voicing repetitive words or by predicting from initial consonants, syntax or semantics: "On Sunday we go to...*church*." Point to specific words while you read with your students, and/or allow them to point themselves. Don't forget that recording students' dictated stories is extremely effective.

BEGINNING READERS

PRAISE AND ENCOURAGE STUDENTS

At this third stage, it is very important to encourage and praise your students as they become more acutely aware of words and struggle to translate the symbols on the page into words and ideas. Never pressure or try to rush your students at this point. Instead, make sure they have adequate prior knowledge of the words, ideas and story line through extensive discussion of the illustrations. It is almost always more effective to teach reading using full sentences. Only in rare cases would it be appropriate to focus a student's attention on an isolated word or sound.

INDEPENDENT READERS

ASSIST STUDENTS TO DEVELOP COMPREHENSION AND RETENTION ABILITIES

As your students graduate to the independent stage of reading, begin to assist them with comprehension and retention by asking pertinent questions. Demonstrate your own reading skills and ability to understand passages by making your students aware of the significant clues that contribute to complete comprehension. Introduce the concept of reading for different purposes: 1) skimming for facts, 2) to find an answer to a question, 3) to learn a new idea, 4) for pleasure, etc.

A tutor points out key words and phrases to aid his student's comprehension.

ALLOW LOTS OF TIME FOR
SILENT READING

Although oral reading is a vehicle for rapid growth in speed and vocabulary, many students find it difficult to attend to meaning during oral sessions and gain comprehension skills primarily through silent reading. Therefore, ensure that silent reading is a significant part of your student's individual reading program. Be prepared to ask your student a number of comprehension questions that are not only factual, but also require the reader to infer, hypothesize and evaluate. If your student has problems with comprehension during this type of reading, demonstrate how you are able to understand a passage by pointing out the key words and phrases that allowed you to grasp the meaning of the reading.

POINT OUT KEY WORDS TO
COMPREHENSION

Teaching Writing

Before you begin to write with your young elementary students, please review Chapter 5 very carefully. It to applies to all writers, young or old.

SCRIBBLING IS AN ATTEMPT TO WRITE

Most children know a great deal about writing even before they arrive at school. Many are immersed in the world of print from earliest childhood: stop signs to shop signs, television guides to labels on store products. That they are very aware of print can be demonstrated by the difference between their drawings and scribbling. Often scribbling is not random; it looks very different from any attempt at picture making. It is "written" in a line from left to right across the page and has the look of writing, with uniform, repetitive shapes of approximately the same size. After they have drawn a picture, many children will respond to your prompting by writing about it and producing these linear left to right doodles. Ask them to read these scribbles to you. Although they may not represent letters, many children can "read" their stories easily. For instance, a drawing of a little dog in front of a house with accompanying scribbles may be read as, "My puppy is waiting for me at the front of my house."

EXPLORE WRITING THROUGH INVENTIVE PLAY

As your young students read with you and see printed words, their scribbles will begin to approximate real letters more and more. Allow them to explore writing through inventive play and practice. As they develop finer motor control, they will begin to make letters or at least better approximations. Make sure you give them the freedom to use inventive spelling as they develop, so they will not hesitate to use their own imaginative, rich oral language. Once these approximations become better, practice letter combinations. Gradually, they will internalize the conventions governing both spelling and writing, and so move on to standardized spelling.

If a child does not want to write, or writes only a very little, it usually is a good indication of a lack of confidence. This must be addressed as the first task. Achieve quantity before you move on to quality.

THROUGH PRACTICE STUDENTS WILL INTERNALIZE WRITING MECHANICS

Always celebrate writing by being a receptive audience and a collaborator in writing who takes pleasure in their efforts and your own. Through constant writing, reading, listening and talking, students will internalize all the forms and mechanics of writing just as surely as you have.

TEACHING SOCIAL SKILLS

YOU ARE AN IMPORTANT ROLE MODEL

Some of your young students may have behaviour patterns that will not allow them to maximize their learning. As a role model, you can teach social skills in both a formal and informal manner. Please review the following list of social skills in relation to your students. Teach those required as a natural part of the whole reading environment during your lessons. Target one skill from this checklist and use strategies to help the student improve.

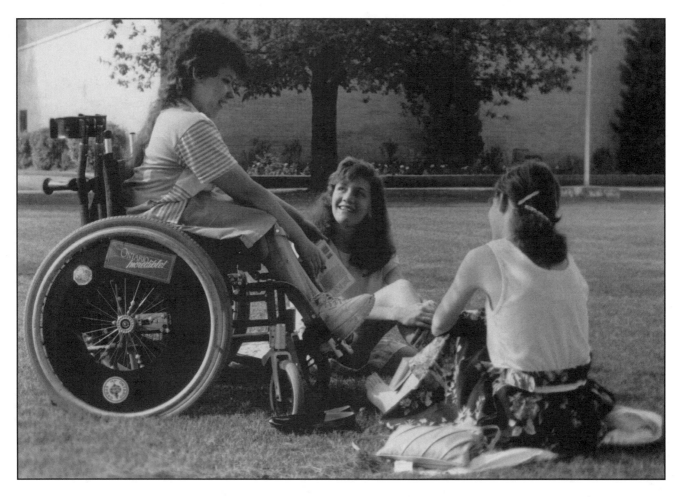

Tutor and students take a break and socialize!

1. Always model the target skill: e.g., Smile and say, "Hello Jimmy."

MODELLING IS THE BEST WAY

2. Use positive reinforcement: e.g., "Great you remembered your book." (Praise.) "When we've finished our reading we'll spend five minutes talking." (Reward.) "It is fun to work with someone who appreciates the help." (Encouragement.)

3. Shaping: e.g., Such behaviours as fidgeting or facial expression indicate the student needs help with a task, but work from the student's current skill level. "I can tell (by the look on your face) you find this difficult. Would you like me to help?"

ENCOURAGE APPROPRIATE RESPONSES

4. Direct instruction: e.g., Don't say: "Listen when I'm talking." Instead, encourage your student to:

   • look at you

   • sit still

   • think about what you say

- nod his or her head/say yes

- respond with a relevant question or comment

As a tutor, be certain you understand and can identify the steps needed to develop the skill in question.

Observe your student's social skills during each tutoring session and keep track of problem areas and improvement using the following checklist.

PREPARE A CHECKLIST FOR YOUR STUDENT

Saying "Hello"				
Never		Sometimes		Always
1	2	3	4	5

1. Saying "Hello:" student responds and initiates greetings with tutor.

2. Saying "Please:" student uses the word please appropriately.

3. Saying "Thank you:" student appreciates tutor's help and says so.

4. Maintains a conversation: student can respond to tutor with more than "yes" or "no."

5. Active listening: student can follow tutor's conversation.

6. Attends to instructions: student can follow tutor's instructions.

7. Brings materials to tutoring session: student remembers to bring a book, pencil, notebook.

ADD TO THIS SUGGESTED CHECKLIST IF NECESSARY

8. Asks for help: student knows when help is needed and asks for it nicely.

9. Asks questions: student knows how and when to ask questions.

10. Ignores distractions: student can concentrate on tutoring despite noisy activities.

11. Sets realistic goals: student chooses an appropriate book.

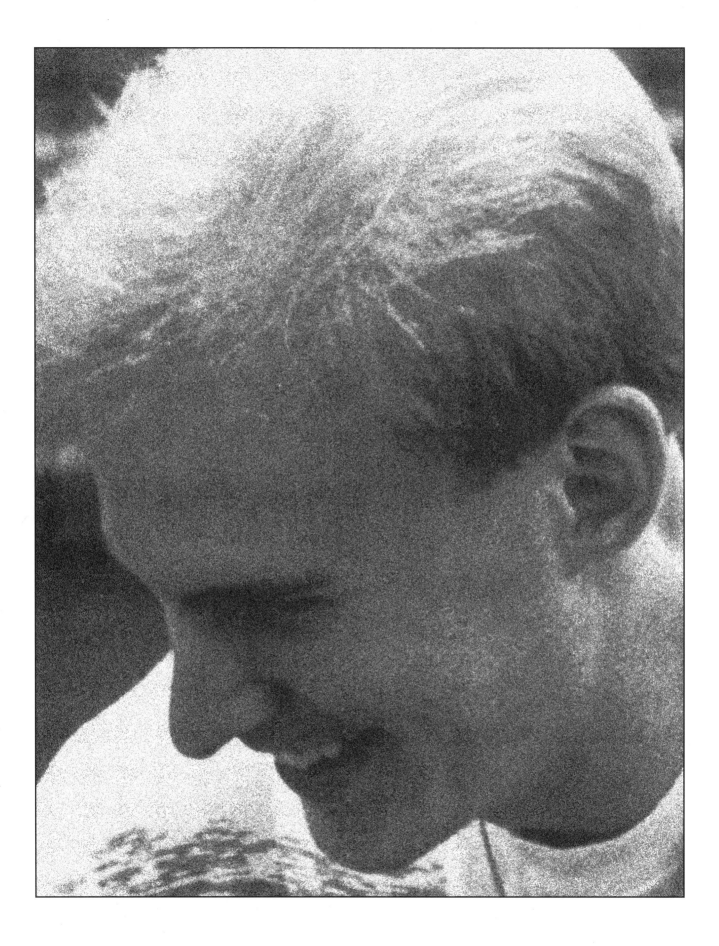

CHAPTER 8

The Art of Listening

ABSOLUTE
COMMUNICATION
IS RARE

ALAS, **R**EAL **C**OMMUNICATION between people is a rare and precious jewel. Often only kindred spirits have it. How many do you know? The poet, John Donne, would have known none if he had written in despair so many centuries ago that we are cut off from each other, rather than saying, "*No* Man is an island unto himself." If we believed we couldn't communicate, then we would have to agree that we live within the prisons of our bodies and the self-imposed barriers of our minds. In this view, no one else can ever truly know us, nor can we, even briefly, truly know another person. Essentially, we are never able to reveal our innermost selves; we live and die alone. Nonsense! Experience shows us otherwise. When communication is absolute, souls can touch. Ask any couple in love.

NO ONE WANTS TO BE
AN "ISLAND"

As we go through life, of course, there are some souls we would rather not touch. No one desires absolute communication with everyone, but you can bet that very few, if any, of us really want to be islands unto ourselves.

Everyone wants some degree of closeness with others. We usually want to have someone with whom we can really and truly share feelings and ideas, but sharing takes skill and practice. Communication of the kindred spirit type requires a maximum of two people: an *intense* speaker and an *avid* listener. It's the only way to bridge those treacherous waters between islands. When people listen well, the barriers come down and closeness develops. As a Reading Tutor this is the kind of atmosphere you want to nurture with your students, because when closeness occurs, they won't be afraid to take risks in reading and writing.

INTENSE SPEAKERS/AVID
LISTENERS COMMUNICATE

Listening well is a sign of respect. It demonstrates to the speaker at the very most, that he or she is important and significant in your life, or at the very least, what is being said is worth considering.

LISTENING IS A SIGN
OF RESPECT

When your student speaks to you, he or she is reaching out. Don't turn away by "turning off" your concentration. Be open. Be considerate. Respond creatively, enthusiastically, with interest. When your student sees you as a good listener, it will follow that you also will be perceived as someone who cares and is interested. This is how you become a "significant other" in your student's eyes. Remember, communication requires a speaker and a listener. When his or her turn comes,

BECOME A SIGNIFICANT
OTHER

Students learn to attend through listening games.

your student will naturally begin to listen just as intently to what you say. Listening is a skill in itself, but it has the added benefit of strengthening the bond between you and your student.

STEPS TOWARD EFFECTIVE LISTENING

The seven steps listed below will help you bridge the communication gap. Practice them until they become a subconscious part of your repertoire.

USE DIRECT EYE CONTACT

1. Move into the speaker's personal space (2-3 feet), once rapport has been developed.

LISTEN INTENTLY

2. Maintain direct eye contact. Don't look at the wall, ceiling, your shoes or a point two feet above the speaker's head. Eye contact indicates interest, openness, trust and a real desire on your part to communicate.

3. Don't formulate an answer, or your own statement on a given topic, while the speaker is talking. If you do, then you won't (can't) listen intently. While you're thinking, you're losing what the speaker is saying at that moment.

ENTHUSIASM CANNOT BE FABRICATED

4. Enthusiasm can't be fabricated. It's genuine only if you are genuinely interested. You can't be genuinely interested in a conversation unless you listen intently.

5. Many people worry about how they sound. As a consequence, they say very little or talk in a stilted fashion. The only way to lose this self-consciousness is to become absorbed in the conversation of another.

BECOME ABSORBED WHILE LISTENING

6. Don't be afraid to let others know who you are. Be open and frank. Respond spontaneously. Look people straight in the eye. Reveal yourself as a person who is interested in other people. Don't worry about your image or making mistakes.

7. Remember, "those who talk, teach/those who listen, learn." If you never listen…?

LISTENING GAMES

These games have been created to develop your listening skills and those of your students. Try them during class, but make sure they remain fun. The object is to improve communication, not win or pass a test.

GAME ONE

USE GROUPS OF THREE

1. Form groups of three: a speaker, a listener and a monitor. The speaker sits directly across from the listener; the monitor sits at right angles to the other two students. Each student will play each of the three roles in turn.

SPEAK FOR TWO MINUTES

2. The speaker is given exactly two minutes to marshal his or her thoughts on a topic provided by the teacher. The speaker must then address the listener continuously for exactly two minutes (use a stop watch). If the speaker has a memory blank, he or she must say "And, and, and" or "But, but, but" so that there are no silences.

3. The listener must give undivided attention to the speaker for those two minutes. At the end of the time, the listener repeats or paraphrases as much as he or she can remember of the speaker's speech.

LISTENER PARAPHRASES SPEAKER

4. The monitor's function is to closely check the listener's paraphrasing of the speaker's conversation.

LISTENER MUST SCORE 80%

If the monitor judges that a listener scores less than 80%, that listener should participate in the following game series. Here, partners are formed with other students who wish to improve their scores.

GAME TWO

1. Using earphones, a partner attends to 15 instructions tape recorded by the other. The speaker must not give the listener any oral clues.

2. The listener's partner scores the student's ability to perform the complete sequence of actions out of a total of fifteen marks.

3. Each partner continues this listening activity over time until each is able to score a perfect mark. Then game one is played again until 80% retention of key ideas is gained.

EASY LISTENING?

One particularly enjoyable—and effective—way to teach listening to students is through old radio programs. These shows from yesteryear are the antithesis of television (primarily a visual medium), because they require careful listening. Radio demands that the imagination provide the visual information to create a picture of the action. The only prompts are the dialogue, the sound effects and music. The only limits are your student's ability to concentrate and create a world in the mind's eye.

RADIO PROGRAMS DEVELOP LISTENING SKILLS AND THE IMAGINATION

You might want to help establish a mood for listening by turning the lights down low, drawing the classroom curtains and presenting *Jack the Ripper* with Vincent Price, or *Dracula*! Expect avid attention and concentration!

Many old radio shows from the 1930s and 40s are readily available at city public libraries. Some of the best enjoyed by students include *Horrific Stories*, by Peter Lorrie; *War of the Worlds*, with Orson Welles; *Boston Blackie*; *The Shadow*; and *The Inner Sanctum* series.

PREPARE QUESTIONS

Develop a minimum of ten questions for any one of these programs. Try to incorporate questions that demand a variety of listening and thinking skills: factual recall, character analysis, plot projection, plot evaluation, hypothesizing outcomes, inferring future actions and so on. You may do this just for your student or together in student-tutor groups. Give the questions in advance if you think you'd like to direct and focus your student's attention. Also consider having students make up ten questions at the end of the program. Tell them in advance, of

ALLOW STUDENTS TO CONSTRUCT QUESTIONS

course, that this is their assignment. You might also ask them to describe what one scene might look like.

Tutors and teacher meet once per week. This is a formal meeting with an agenda

USE RADIO SHOWS DURING TUTOR-TEACHER MEETINGS

Radio shows may be used once per week during teacher-tutor weekly meetings. Tutors in rotation can supervise students collectively and receive the meeting's minutes at a later date. If students listen to just one radio program per week, you will find a measurable increase in his or her listening, thinking and writing skills, as well as a marked difference in imaginative creative abilities.

Overall, keep in mind that many of your students may have had difficulty with reading and writing in the past because they have not listened, or been listened to, effectively. Your study of the art of listening will go a long way toward bringing them the confidence and the success they deserve.

CHAPTER 9

Helping with Subjects

AS A TUTOR, YOUR MAJOR CONCERN and first priority is always to guide your student toward acquiring the basics of reading and writing. However, because they have low skill levels, many students also will have difficulty with regular classroom work, especially texts written at their frustration level. Depending upon the requirements of the individual student, you may choose to use up to half of any tutoring session in assisting with classroom subjects: homework, in-class assignments and reading subject texts.

*Nevertheless, it is very important that you **never** go beyond half of a session on these activities. The reason is simple. The frustration for an underachieving student caused by trying to read classroom texts for the full session will inhibit progress in basic reading and writing. Although better subject marks may seem to be the result of your extensive help with subjects in the short term, the situation is really artificial. If you go beyond the half-session rule, you simply will be acting as a crutch. Remove your support, and your student will fall to his or her former level in class. Far better to strive for long term gains in reading and writing. In the end, the whole purpose of the Reading Tutor Program is to wean your students from needing you at all. Your job, in a way, is to make yourself unnecessary for an individual student by making him or her self-sufficient.*

Even so, you can offer some important assistance to your students in subject areas. You attend senior advanced level classes. As such, you are an expert in most subjects in the eyes of the junior grade or skill-deficient students you are tutoring. Beyond this, it is very likely that you have felt some of the frustration they do when approaching a text that is very difficult to read. Translate this experience, this "I know, I've been there" idea, into concrete assistance.

Begin in practical areas. Teach your students how to "rewrite" basic concepts in their own words. Help them practice taking notes. Show them how to write precisely. Remember, teachers are the expert instructors, but you are the excellent learner. Tutor your student in the wide range of strategies for learning and doing well that are responsible for your school success.

You have a distinct advantage in this kind of tutoring. You have spent one or more years steeping yourself in math, English, science,

---

TEXTS MAY BE AT FRUSTRATION LEVELS

NEVER GO BEYOND HALF PERIOD TIME FRAMES WITH SUBJECT ASSISTANCE

DON'T BE JUST A CRUTCH

THE GOAL IS SELF-SUFFICIENCY

TUTORS ARE EXPERTS IN SUBJECT AREAS

The tutor and her student discuss the content of the science text.

geography and many other subjects at a much more difficult level than your student. You have your strengths, no doubt, and you should let the teacher know what they are; they may determine who you will tutor. If one of your best subjects is science, for example, you may be assigned to a student who needs help in that area.

INFORM READING TEACHER OF YOUR SUBJECT STRENGTHS

Study the six strategies listed below. They will help you assist your students in any subject.

1. Keep in contact with your student's subject teacher.

2. Ask the teacher to let you know when the student's major assignments are due and the dates of quizzes and tests. You might want to step up your assistance at those times.

CONTACT SUBJECT TEACHERS AT FIRST OPPORTUNITY

3. You also should know about major homework, essays, projects and presentations. Ask the student's subject teacher to relay the necessary information to you via your homeroom teacher's mailbox (Often the homeroom teacher for tutors is their classroom teacher for this course).

CHECK YOUR STUDENT'S
SUBJECT NOTES

4. The quality of his or her subject notes accounts for 20 per cent of the student's mark. Review your student's binder and notebook at least once every two weeks or so to ensure that assignments are complete and in order.

5. Remember, many subject texts are written at your student's frustration level. When he or she is absent, you may want to spend the time tape recording core subject texts at a speed sufficiently slow to aid in comprehension. Summarize key concepts on the tape before continuing to record the text. If several tutors use this approach over time, a substantial library of recorded texts can be developed at your school. Your student should use these tapes in a listen and read format.

RECORD SUBJECT TEXTS

6. Tell your student to read the questions listed at the end of a chapter before reading the text. This strategy helps add focus to the reading.

YOU CAN OFFER YOUR
STUDENT A FULL SUPPORT
SYSTEM

Tutoring younger students in subjects you know well may give you a great deal of pleasure. Even with subjects you haven't studied, you can still be of great assistance by helping with text reading, defining major concepts and note taking. ***Just keep in mind that your major task as a Reading Tutor is to instill the basics of reading and writing, so don't exceed the half-session rule.*** In the end, you will be able to take real pride in giving your student the full support he or she need to succeed in school.

CHAPTER 10

Tutoring in Mathematics

Most teachers are specialists who have developed expertise in specific subject areas and who may often teach only in that realm. By contrast, as a senior student you are a generalist, and so you have developed considerable knowledge in most of the major subjects. Thus, you will have little difficulty in assisting junior students in courses with which they are experiencing difficulty or failure.

READING AND MATH PROBLEMS MOST COMMON

While schools cover a wide variety of subjects, it is a general truth that the two most common problem areas for students are reading and mathematics. This is a special chapter on tutoring in mathematics. What follows is designed to be of practical interest to those tutors who have been assigned students with moderate difficulty in math. It should be of significant use for those tutors providing intensive tutoring in this subject.

MATH EXPERTS ARE IN THE CLASS

Indeed for this program, some tutors have been selected because they enjoy mathematics and excel in it. They are the classroom experts in this subject. If you and your student encounter difficulty, consult one of these experts, just as you would seek assistance from those tutors in the classroom who excel in other subject areas.

MEET THE MATH TEACHER

When you are assigned a student for math tutoring, the first thing you should do is make an appointment with your student's math teacher. Ask for a list of the concepts and skills which must be learned by your student in order to earn credit. As a result of your interview with the teacher and a careful analysis of the student's strengths and weaknesses, you should be able to develop an accurate profile of your student's attitude towards and ability in mathematics. Benchmark evaluation will be of great assistance in this task.

Is you student working below standard. Does he or she have a serious lack of basic arithmetic skills, concepts and vocabulary? Is there a corresponding lack of confidence in his or her own ability?

DEVELOP-SHORT AND LONG TERM GOALS FROM STUDENT DATA

To prepare the profile you should review samples of the exercises, tests and homework of your student. Based on this data try to develop goals you would like your student to achieve, goals that apply both to the short term and the long term. These may be goals set to help the learner gain confidence, to improve his or her skills to the appropriate level, and to acquire a level of competency in math to meet everyday needs. Continue to seek imput from the student's teacher when necessary.

Math teachers despair, when students won't ask questions

QUESTION AND
ANSWER FORMAT

BEGIN AT
INDEPENDENT LEVEL

In my interviews with teachers and tutors, I have discovered that many students are often embarrassed to ask questions in math class for fear of looking less capable than others. This attitude makes math teachers despair because math is not a subject that is learned by lecture format. There must be constant dialogue between teacher and student: the question and answer format is necessary to acquire the concepts and sequential steps involved for the development of a solid base of knowledge in mathematics. As in reading, students must have an appropriate experiential base for success.

It is crucially important to make every effort to instill your student with confidence. The student needs encouragement and specific help to overcome the mental blocks he or she may have. At the same time it is essential to begin your tutoring at your student's *independent* math level. Work first at what your student can do well. This will do much to put a student at ease and help him or her to build the confidence necessary to engage the new concepts that lie ahead when you begin working at your student's *instructional* level.

STUDENTS'S PRIOR
KNOWLEDGE

IS STUDENT
EXPERIENTAL BASE
APPROPRIATE

DIAGNOSTIC MATH
TEST FROM TEACHER

PRACTICE MAKES
PERFECT

DISCREET LEARNING
IS BEST

MATH BASED ON
SEQUENTIAL STEPS

As you know comprehension is a function of an individual's prior knowledge. Certainly, mathematics is built on a base of fundamental knowledge; hence, intensive review and practice at the independent level will greatly enhance your student's success rate at the instructional level.

Because students have to apply prior knowledge to understand new concepts, make sure that their experiential base is appropriate for the new material ahead. Remember that, as in reading, the surface structure of meaning (the minimal information) is on the page ; however, the deep structure of meaning must be in the mind of the students if they are to comprehend adequately.

Before moving to the instructional level, you will want to determine if your student has a sufficient mathematical background to apply to new learning. Use a diagnostic test obtained from the mathematics teacher to determine your student's level of ability and specific needs. Once you know what these needs are, establish a schedule to meet them. Your goal is to have your student achieve mastery over a set of particular skills before moving on.

Once a concept is mastered by your student, help him or her retain it by preparing exercises which offer practice in the newly acquired skill. Emphasize that in mathematics especially, "practice makes perfect."

Speak with the math teacher about establishing a procedure for measuring your student's progress and proficiency. Use math benchmarks or standards if possible. If you find it necessary, ask if you can modify exercises in your student's text to better serve his or her particular needs.

By the time you begin to move on to your student's instructional level, you will probably have formed a bond and a level of trust with your student. An important plus in your relationship—and a significant advantage you have over a classroom teacher—is that you will be constantly working on a one-to-one basis over the term. This is discreet learning, for your student does not face the embarrassment of having the whole class hear his or her answers.

At the instructional level seek to develop your student's abilities carefully by setting up increments or units of learning. Make it clear that mathematical problems are based on sequential steps. One step is predicated on another. Miss one, and the answer will be impossible to achieve. This is true whether you are working with your student on basic multiplication and division or on complex algebraic equations.

Always set new goals based on a careful assessment of your student's current ability. When working at the instructional level, pick exercises related to the new material from your student's textbook that he or she is capable of doing. Build new lessons on previous tutoring sessions.

Mathematics is learning by doing

WATCH STUDENT
DO THE WORK

HELP STUDENT
VISUALIZE SOLUTIONS

Mathematics is "learning by doing." *Thus spend much more time watching your student work out a solution to a math question than telling him or her how to do it.* Active involvement by your student is the glue of retention. You may well observe that your student knows how to do most of a math problem but is missing just one or two key steps in order to arrive at the successful solution. Only through close observation will you realize this is the case.

Whenever possible, map or illustrate mathematical concepts to help your student visualize how a solution can be reached. Use the wedge of a pie to demonstrate fractions of a whole. Money can be an effective medium in teaching addition, subtraction, multiplication, and division. Concrete examples allow students to view mathematics as an essential subject pertinent to their everyday needs.

Triangulation in geometry can be taught by applying these concepts to real-life situations. For example, foresters measure the height of a tree by running out a baseline of one hundred feet from the trunk. At that distance, they next read the angle from the bottom of the tree to its top and calculate the height. If surveyors couldn't calculate the dis-

Students relate new concepts to prior knowledge

**NEED MATH FOR
EVERYDAY NEEDS**

tance over a river, they might have to boat over dangerous water. Certainly, its easier to calculate the distance up a steep cliff than to climb it!

Fill a glass jar with marbles. Set up a contest to determine the number of marbles in the jar. Develop a formula to find out, perhaps one using weight as the means. The more you use puzzles, games, newspapers, magazines, and sports to build interest and add variety to math lessons, the greater will be your student's enjoyment, as he or she begins to realize the practical application of mathematical skills to everyday life.

**BUILD INTEREST AND
ADD VARIETY**

If your student doesn't understand a solution, perhaps he or she doesn't have sufficient prior knowledge (the deep structure of meaning) to understand the surface structure of the new math problem on the page. Review the basic skills and concepts which bear on the question at hand. As in reading, students will learn new mathematical information by relating it to old information. As noted once before Robert Frost said, "We learn by metaphor." Your student will have to relate new concepts to the prior knowledge in his or her experiential

**RELATE NEW
MATH TO OLD**

base, which must be adequate, if he or she is to "see" the solution to a brand new type of problem.

BREAK PROBLEMS INTO MANAGEABLE CHUNKS

When your student encounters what seems to be a complex problem, break it down into manageable chunks. In that way, students are not intimidated by the whole thing at once ; instead, they begin to see the components in sequence. When skiing a steep incline, a look down the whole slope or mountain can be intimidating. However, break that mountain down into short runs and the challenge can be met with ease and confidence, leaving skiers to wonder why they thought it overwhelming in the first place!

INCREMENTAL STEPS LEAD TO SUCCESS

Make sure you praise your student for work well done. Be encouraging,while avoiding false praise: it will work wonders, if the student begins to believe that he or she can be "good" in this subject. Never jump ahead of your student's current ability to understand. Keep to the necessary incremental steps.

USE YOUR OWN WORDS

When describing how to complete a mathematical operation, tell your student in your own words the steps involved, or how you understand a specific concept. The more individualized and informal the tutorial session is, the better it will be for your student. While you will likely rely on your student's classroom textbook to a great degree, supplement it by using your own illustrations and examples of the work.

EVALUATION IS IMPORTANT

Evaluation of the student's progress is an important component of the process. In their regular math course students will be writing tests and quizzes to determine individual progress. Help them prepare: find out what the tests will measure. Has your student mastered the necessary skills for success?

REVIEW FOR TEST WELL IN ADVANCE

Start a review for a forthcoming test or quiz several days in advance and go over any problems with which your student has had difficulty. Use examples from previous work related to the coming test. Does your student know the definitions required? Does he or she understand them? Perhaps give your student a similar pre-test, but first check with the math teacher to ensure your test adequately measures the skills in question.

KEEP A JOURNAL

Don't forget to keep a careful journal of your student's activities, just as you would when tutoring in reading. Indicate the mathematical concepts and skills mastered and those not mastered. Note your student's level of confidence and enjoyment during the various sessions. All the data in your journal will be beneficial to you as a source of information when you write your student profiles.

FORMATIVE/SUMMATIVE STUDENT PROFILES REQUIRED

The formative student profile written by math tutors should describe the student's ability at the time of writing: his or her strengths, difficulties, accomplishments, and the concepts and skills yet to be mastered. The summative profile at the end of the semester or school year should indicate the learning outcomes: your student's growth in different areas accomplished over the term. Use benchmarks or standards to

YOUR OWN MATH
SKILLS WILL IMPROVE

assist your profile development. Include references to skills, concepts, attitude, and degree of confidence. Is your student now at grade level in mathematics? Does your student demonstrate sufficient organizational skills and study habits? These profiles, while marked by your teacher, should be forwarded to your student's mathematics teacher for his or her files.

Above all, enjoy tutoring in math. As in tutoring in reading and writing, there is an important side benefit: your own skills and enjoyment will increase in this subject area as you interact with and assist your student. Ask any teacher: there is no better way to learn a subject well than to instruct in it!

TIPS FOR TUTORS

- establish an appropriate setting with proper equipment available

-help build a positive attitude - "Attitude is Everything"

- begin each session by recalling skills and concepts from the previous day

-begin at the student's independent level of instruction

- never work at your student's frustrational level

- students must be able to apply prior knowledge to understand new concepts; make sure your student's experiential base is in "synch" with the new material to be learned.

- use examples that are familiar to the student

- illustrate math concepts by practical examples when possible

- break complex problems down into manageable chunks

- use "hands-on" materials, including calculators, whenever possible

- don't forget to use math puzzles and games

- include the use of newspapers, magazines, and sports for variety and interest

- demonstrate the appropriate use of calculators to eliminate tedious calculations

- stress constant practice in order to master basic skills.

- base the marks or grades you give on improvement in skills

- use benchmark evaluation

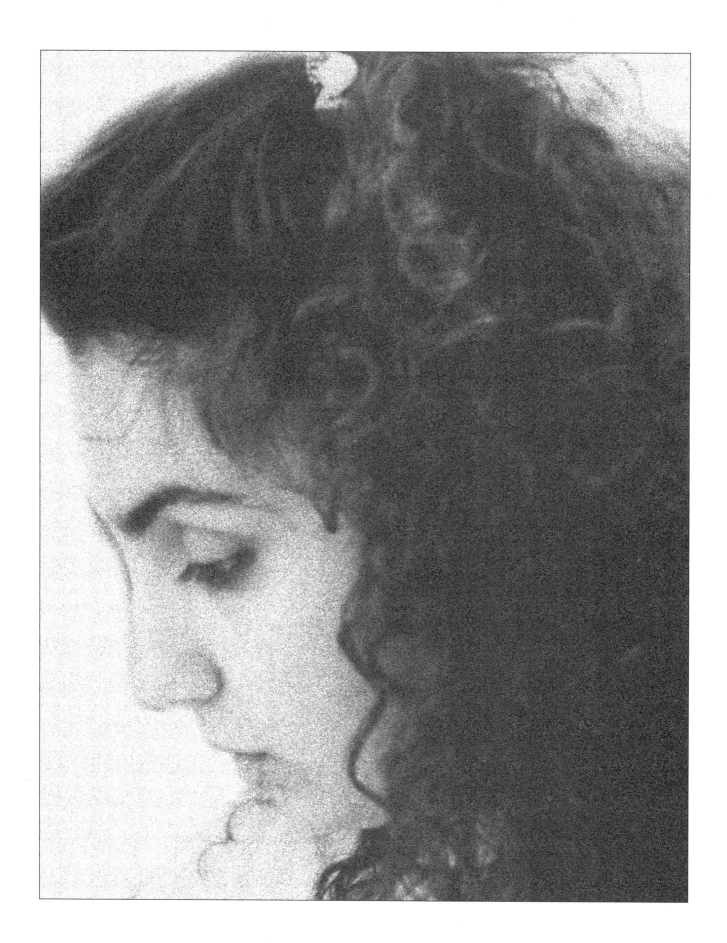

CHAPTER 11

The Tutor as Mentor

ONE OF YOUR MOST important functions as a Reading Tutor is to act as a mentor, an experienced and trusted adviser for your students. You are experienced academically. You know the ropes, the way to achieve success in school. Your students don't. Most often they find school intimidating and worry about failure, about ending up at the bottom of the heap.

OPPORTUNITY TO FORM A CLOSE RELATIONSHIP

You have an excellent chance to form a close relationship with an individual student. Unlike a teacher, your contact with your student is one-to-one. Younger students will tend to look up to and admire older tutors as big brothers or big sisters. This is the kind of situation that many younger students desire but sometimes won't admit. Once such a relationship is established, you are well on your way to becoming a trusted mentor, perhaps the only one the student wants.

BE A BIG BROTHER/ BIG SISTER

Effective mentoring begins in the one-to-one relationship with your student. One is helped; the other is helping. So long as each person treats the other with respect, as an equal, a bond should form that is pleasing to both of you. In most cases, you and your student will be relatively near in age, and you will be viewed as someone from the same "world" who shares attitudes about music, clothes, food, films and so on.

GENUINE FRIENDSHIPS MAY HAPPEN

Your obligation actually goes no further than gaining a course credit as a Reading Tutor. However, if a genuine friendship develops, allow it. At some schools, tutors and students have gone on fishing trips or to dinner at each other's homes. One eighteen year old tutor took his thirteen year old student to see her first play. Another took her student to the zoo. We all can detect insincerity; only engage in activities like these if you both really want to have a friendship. No matter how you approach it, mentoring is a social activity. Enjoy it!

READING ROOM CAN BECOME A QUASI CLUB OR SAFE HAVEN

In many schools, students have become friends or acquaintances with tutors other than their own. The Reading Room can become a sort of club or safe haven where such relationships can flower, because students will tend to drop in at times other than scheduled sessions to chat or read quietly. Regular desks for working and comfortable chairs for reading can establish a casual, friendly, helping environment that encourages camaraderie.

This student enjoys his special relationship with his tutor.

Beyond this general outline, being a mentor involves both the formal and informal responsibilities listed below. Read them over. Follow them. They have benefits for you and your student.

FORMAL MENTORING

- Maintain contact with your students' subject teachers. How are they relating? How are they doing?

- Encourage students to come to you with problems or concerns, especially if their relationship has been poor with adults.

SHARE SERIOUS INFORMATION WITH RESPONSIBLE OTHERS

- Most of what you learn in the tutor-student relationship is private and for your ears only. However, in serious circumstances, never make a decision about your student on your own. Share the information and decision process with your teacher or Guidance person. No one wants to shoulder the burden of a bad decision alone, so don't place yourself in a legal position of having counselled someone on your own.

- Periodically check your student's attendance.

- Speak to attendance counsellors about significant absences.

- After training, some schools allow tutors to call home about absences and to inform parents of the support they offer.

CALL PARENTS WITH GOOD NEWS

- Call sometimes with just the good news. "Julie's reading is up." "Johnny likes his classes now." Parents are pleased to be informed of their youngster's progress.

- Defend your student when there is just cause, but make sure you have all the facts first.

DEFEND STUDENT WHEN CAUSE IS JUST; GET THE FACTS FIRST

- Some school's committees may seek input from tutors before making decisions on a student's future course. If this is the case in your school, bring documentation: writing samples, student profiles, reading test results and journals.

DISCUSS MENTORING AT WEEKLY MEETINGS

- Discuss your role as a mentor at weekly meetings. If the relationship is not going well after a significant period of time, tell the teacher. In some cases, good relationships just won't form. It will probably be no one's fault, but the support of a professional could be crucial. Don't feel you have to go it alone. Such may be detrimental for you and your student.

- Establish the boundaries of mentoring. Don't let it go beyond the limits with which you are comfortable.

- Be a positive role model.

Conversation among friends.

INFORMAL MENTORING

- Say "hello" in the halls.

- Have "rap" sessions when time permits. Tell the student about your interests and ask about his or hers.

TRY A VARIETY OF FRIENDLY ACTIVITIES

- Attempt to be that big brother or big sister. Respect, admire and share fun!

- Introduce your student to your friends.

- Encourage your student to join school clubs and teams.

- Let your students cheer you on in school sports or other activities. Let them know you'd like their support!

- Often students will invite their tutors to formal school dinners, rather than teachers or friends. Go! It's free food!

SPREAD THE WORD THAT YOUR STUDENTS ARE FINE

- If you feel like it, have lunch with your student in the cafeteria.

- If you like your students and think they're fine, spread the word.

- Look out for them.

- Demonstrate other ways of acting and viewing the world and those in it.

- If your student's parents are neighbours, casually say hello once in a while.

YOU CAN MAKE A POWERFUL, POSITIVE IMPACT

Above all, bear in mind that as a trusted adviser you can have a powerful positive impact on your student that goes well beyond your influence as a Reading Tutor. This is an awesome responsibility. It's also a challenge. Ultimately, it can be quite rewarding.

CHAPTER 12

Duties and Evaluation

THROUGHOUT **T**HE **Y**EAR, the Reading Tutor will be required to carry out a number of assignments related directly to his or her secondary or elementary student. You will be evaluated, in part, on your ability to fulfill these requirements and on passing a test based on this manual with an average of 75 per cent.

TUTORS HAVE A NUMBER OF IMPORTANT ASSIGNMENTS AND DUTIES

Initially, you must interview your student. At the beginning and end of the year, you may mark pre-program and post-program reading evaluations with the teacher's assistance.

As the program progresses, you will be required to keep weekly anecdotal reports or journals on your student. (You will be given time in class for this activity.) During weekly meetings, you will be expected to cite items from your journal concerning your student's progress.

MAINTAIN A NUMBER OF DIFFERENT RECORDS

Records must be kept of writing, assisted homework and assignments in the folder you make up for your student. Also, you should record day-to-day informal observations on progress (see Appendix A for assessment sheets). As well, you will be required to maintain student profiles and keep copies of the self-evaluations completed by the student.

At the secondary level, your formal evaluation will be determined by the teacher responsible for this program based on the following criteria. With elementary students, however, the teachers responsible for your students will be involved too.

TUTOR EVALUATION

Your formal evaluation will be based on the following criteria:

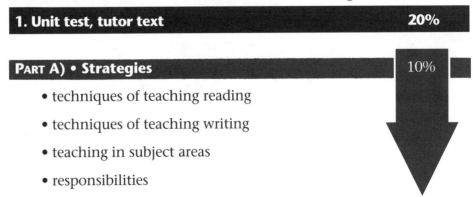

| 1. Unit test, tutor text | 20% |

| PART A) • Strategies | 10% |

- techniques of teaching reading
- techniques of teaching writing
- teaching in subject areas
- responsibilities

THE MANUAL TEST IS VALUED AT 20%

Collaboration is one of the best methods of teaching writing.

- reading material
- mentoring
- behaviour modification techniques
- listening techniques

PART B) • case study of a student who needs help reading   10%

2. Attendance and effort: 20%

GOOD ATTENDANCE
IS A MUST

- daily attendance
- enthusiasm and commitment
- daily preparation

3. Student profiles: 10%

SUBMIT AT LEAST TWO
STUDENT PROFILES
PER TERM

- formative profile (mid term)   } If possible, use benchmark
- summative profile (end of term) } evaluation to develop both
                                     profiles.

WEEKLY JOURNALS
SUBMITTED REGULARLY

4. Tutor's journal: 10%

- mid-term
- end of semester

5. Testing and conferences: 10%

SIT EXAMS AND
ADMINISTER EVALUATIONS

- administering and marking pre-program reading evaluations
- administering and marking post-program reading evaluations
- conferences with student's subject teachers
- sitting one final exam with student
- generating student's tentative mid-term and final marks

6. Effectiveness: 10%

CONFERENCE WITH
SUBJECT TEACHERS

- how well the tutor attempted to meet the learning needs of the skill-deficient student:

DEVELOP ALL THE
ATTRIBUTES OF A
STRONG TUTOR

a) motivation

b) rapport

c) enthusiasm

d) sensitivity to student

e) responsibility

7. The final is a three-part exam: 20%

WRITE LETTER TO THE
TUTOR FOR NEXT YEAR

a) Write a letter to your student's tutor for next year. Describe your student's attitudes, strengths, weaknesses, likes, dislikes, progress, favourite books, instructional level, etc. Describe how best to serve this student.

EVALUATE PROGRAM

b) Write an evaluation of the Reading Tutor Program. Suggest improvement where necessary or additional techniques of teaching reading and writing not included in this text.

c) A self-evaluation:

- personal benefits of the course

WHAT DID YOU LEARN?

- qualities and skills gained
- phases of tutoring that you're good at
- areas which you would like to improve
- indicate learning that's taken place for you

TOTAL 100%

The tutor and her student enjoy a book together.

STATEMENTS OF GROWTH
FOR YOUR STUDENT AND
YOU

You will not be evaluated on an absolute standard relating to your student's improvement. That would be most unfair, for people learn at different rates. It is expected, however, that the student will show some improvement. For this reason, we will rely to some extent on your and your student's self-evaluations as effective statements of growth and achievement for both of you.

STUDENT ASSESSMENT

HOW EFFECTIVE IS THE
PROGRAM FOR
YOUR STUDENT?

Student assessment is necessary for a number of reasons. Foremost, it is an objective method of demonstrating to students their growth in communication skills. Students will feel positive when told of gains in reading and writing, especially if the improvements are greater than in the past. Furthermore, assessment lets both tutors and teachers know the effectiveness of individualized programs. Finally, because the tutoring program is fully individualized and at appropriate instructional levels for all students, there is a clear opportunity for excellent marks. That is, students are not marked against an absolute standard but on the basis of individual improvement. High marks are positive motivation.

Tutors and students participate in reading the script of a film.

A method of student evaluation has been developed called benchmarks or standards. They are samples of students' work on a wide range of language and mathematics tasks. These samples show what various students can accomplish on learning tasks and are usually divided into a range of levels of student performance. Benchmarks indicate how well a student is doing: the current level of his or her achievement.

The main idea behind the use of benchmarks is that learning is developmental, as are reading and writing skills. Thus, they are used to improve students' skills. By looking at outcomes, the work students produce, tutors can find out what level their student is at and then help the student move on to the next level of ability or performance. Never jump a level: progress through the levels in developmental fashion, thereby helping your student maximize his or her potential. Learning outcomes are valuable tools to further develop your student's problem solving ability, higher level thinking and communication skills.

Benchmarks can truly individualize your student's program, so that he or she won't be marked against others in the class or an absolute standard but on their individual improvement over time. If they are available, use them to move your student along the path to excellence!

A final draft is typed on the word processor.

FORMAL TESTS ARE NOT AS VALID AS TUTOR'S EVALUATION

You will certainly want to know how your students are progressing as you tutor them. Your own formal and informal, daily observations of your student's growth are really far more valid than the results of any standardized test. Assess your student's gains and current level of performance in reading regularly.

An example, if a story to be read is about Panda Bears, do the following in order. Before your student reads, discuss the story incorporating significant words that will have to be read: Panda, China, extinct, bamboo, etc, and also the basic concepts in the story. Ask for a general description of Pandas. Does he or she know they're from China and in danger of becoming extinct, or that they eat bamboo? Allow your student to guess what information will be in the story. Then allow him or her to read it while you record the reading time. Next, allow your student to write about the significant aspects of the story. Finally, find out if your student thought that reading and writing about Pandas was easy.

JOURNALS ARE THE SOURCE MATERIAL FOR STUDENT PROFILES

Rate all of this process; pre-reading, reading, writing, your student's response and his or her evaluation of the story on a scale of one to ten. Make sure to record these observations in your weekly journal which must be submitted for evaluation. Your journals, of course, are a source when writing your student's profile.

Obviously, writing growth can be assessed overall by contrasting the very first draft your student wrote at the beginning of the year and a current piece. Show your student both the "before" and the "after." The student is the one who must know he or she can improve to internalize that belief.

All students will require tutoring five days per week, and they will earn a full credit for their efforts. In reality, this is often their most important course in school because it directly attacks the root cause of their inability to succeed in their other subject areas.

As a specific student's tutor, you will probably be the one person most familiar with his or her gains in all aspects of communication. Certainly, you will be more acutely aware of your student's progress than your supervising teacher who will be overseeing a great number of students: both tutors and, collectively, tutors' students at the same time.

Your student will be awarded his or her mid-term and final mark based on the following criteria: Reading-Skill Improvement, Writing Skill Improvement, Subject-Notebook Quality, Attendance and Attitude. Each component is valued at 20 per cent. At mid-term and the end of the year, you will make up a final mark sheet and a comprehensive anecdotal report on your student (see Appendix A).

Reading Skill Improvement. Indicate the student's growth in vocabulary, comprehension and reading speed. These observations should be gleaned both from current reading assessments and your own observations and opinions. Again, your own opinion is more valid than standardized reading test results.

Writing Skill Improvement. Submit a copy of the student's first piece of writing and a current draft to substantiate your written assessment. Comment on style, coherence, clarity, punctuation, sentence structure and cursive writing ability.

Subject-Notebook Quality. Indicate the quality of organization and neatness of the student's notes. The mark, however, is mainly dependent on the completeness of the notes. Deduct marks for missing assignments, notes from the board, homework, etc.

Attendance. Subtract one mark per absence, other than those covered by a doctor's or parents' statement of illness or those caused by legitimate school activities.

Attitude. The student who demonstrates a positive attitude, a desire to learn and a willingness to develop excellent rapport with you deserves full marks.

Tutors will be given class time at mid-term and at the end of the year to have a fifteen minute conference with the supervising teacher to determine the student's report card mark. Please have sufficient documentation to substantiate your appraisal. While tutors obviously have significant impact in determining the student's assessment, the teacher has the final authority.

THIS IS AN IMPORTANT CLASS FOR YOUR STUDENT

YOU WILL BE MOST AWARE OF STUDENT GAINS

THE CRITERIA IS SKILL BASED

NOTE READING GROWTH

DEMONSTRATE WRITING GROWTH

HOW COMPLETE ARE SUBJECT NOTES?

TEACHER-TUTOR CONFERENCE A MUST!

TEACHER HAS FINAL AUTHORITY

"The Most Honourable Profession"

THAT'S WHAT SOCRATES SAID of teaching. And he was right, because teaching is the most honourable of professions, *when it makes a difference*. You can make that difference in your student's life.

Certainly, I find teaching reading to young students more gratifying than anything else I've ever done, despite the occasional headaches. I'm convinced that you, as a hand-picked member of a select group of reading tutors, will do well and make a difference.

YOU CAN MAKE A DIFFERENCE

Many tutors don't consider their own marks the first priority. Tutoring itself is the primary concern. Seen in this way, the relationship with your student is the most important ingredient for success. Don't worry about occasional mistakes. The one-to-one format is the best teaching strategy. Your student needs support, and your presence alone will do much to meet that need. If your student knows you care, he or she will make the effort and have the courage to try.

ONE-TO-ONE FORMAT IS THE BEST TEACHING METHOD

You have the ability to develop a unique reading program tailor-made for your student. What could be better for him or her? Contact with you and continuous reading and writing will bring your student the real and vicarious knowledge needed to broaden his or her experiential base. What you can offer your students, then, is an enhanced ability to comprehend what is read and, consequently, the world around them.

You may very well succeed where others have failed. Simply by teaching the essential skills of reading and writing, you can radically change a student's life forever. You can open doors to a decent future. You can infuse your student with self-worth and self-esteem. You can give back the sense of dignity that was lost so long ago.

YOUR EFFORTS CAN HELP RADICALLY CHANGE A STUDENT'S LIFE FOR THE BETTER

What's in it for you? Much more than a credit, because you will find a solid core of integrity that nothing can assail. This is probably the most valuable personal attribute you can ever have. I'm sure you will do well. You have great skills, strengths, sensitivity and intuition about teaching or you would not be in this class. I hope you enjoy this course and find it as personally rewarding as my tutors do. Have fun and remember that we believe in you, so believe in yourself!

DEVELOP SOLID INTEGRITY

ABOVE ALL, ENJOY THIS COURSE!

Sample Records

INITIAL LETTER FROM A TUTOR
TO A STUDENT'S SUBJECT TEACHER

Dear Mr. R_____,

I would like you to know that I am Jimmy B_____'s reading tutor this semester. I will be working with him five days per week during period one. Most of my time will be spent improving Jimmy's reading and writing skills. However, **some** of the period will be used to assist him in subject areas. Please let me know through my homeroom when he has major tests and quizzes, and I will help him prepare.

Feel free to send along any assignments or homework that he has difficulty with. If I may, I would like to meet with you periodically over the term to discuss his progress in your class. Thank you for your co-operation.

Sincerely,

Mary T_____

Reading Tutor

TUTOR'S RECORD OF ASSISTANCE IN SUBJECT AREAS

To be submitted monthly to subject teachers.

When helping students in subject areas, only assist when necessary so that completed assignments are the products of the students' **own knowledge, beliefs and attitudes**. In other words, help only to the extent that allows them to gain an effective medium of communication for the expression of their subject knowledge. Keep copies of these records for your files.

---

1. Assistance in Subject Readings   Date: _____

Details: a)

b)

c)

---

2. Assistance in Subject Writing (Projects, Essays) Date: _____

Details: a)

b)

c)

---

3. Homework Assistance   Date: _____

Details: a)

b)

c)

STUDENT PROFILES

You will write student profiles in anecdotal form without subheadings. (see the following example) The specifics of these profiles are mandatory for mid-term and end of term. Your evaluations should be detailed and comprehensive, and if possible, include the use of benchmarks or standards to determine the current level of your student's performance.

STUDENT'S NAME: _____

TUTOR: _____

SKILLS:

1) Reading: (comment on progress, speed, vocabulary and comprehension)

----

2) Writing: letter formation, spelling, coherence, etc.

STUDENT'S ABILITY TO COPE EFFECTIVELY IN SUBJECT AREAS:
Comment on the following: engagement of texts, comprehension of assignments, ability to complete work, (i.e., speed/time factor), and ability to engage unit and final tests.

STUDENT ATTITUDE: Positive/negative, problems.

TEACHING STRATEGIES: Suggestions on how this student would best be assisted at this school.

OTHER PERTINENT OBSERVATIONS:

A TUTOR'S JOURNAL ENTRY ABOUT A
STUDENT WITH SIGNIFICANT DIFFICULTIES

The student with whom I have been working has a history, especially in school settings, of being extremely difficult to manage. For this reason, he now finds himself, at age sixteen, with no completed high school credits to his name. In fact, this semester is the first time in two years that he has been enrolled in school. Needless to say, his chances have not been viewed optimistically by the administration, who have based their opinion, and time will tell how rightly, on his past poor performance and behaviour problems.

As one who has worked with this student on an individual basis, it seems clear to me that these problems do not reflect his true potential. While the administration has my sympathy, I feel it quite unfortunate that this student was not given the opportunity to learn in a one-to-one instructional environment with someone whom he did not perceive as being part of the system that, inadvertently, had made him feel inadequate for so long. I recognize that many fine teachers have sacrificed a great deal of their spare time to help this student. I am not saying that they failed, but perhaps someone to sit in the desk beside him, and not in the desk in front of him, would meet with less resistance.

The question now is have we intervened too late: (R_____ is sixteen?)

R_____ has expressed keenly the desire to learn. However, perhaps years of calloused stereotyping and what he perceives as apparent lack of concern by others have forced him to build up barriers that must constantly be battled.

This challenge, in my opinion, cannot be met by teachers in classroom situations, no matter how concerned or determined they might be.

Already this year, R_____ has stayed in school longer than most predicted and has earned respectable grades as well. This is not to say that the war has been won, but it is a clear indication that this program can at least begin to succeed where years of the traditional system have not.

STUDENT ASSESSMENT SHEET

MARKS CHART

Submitted twice per term with supporting evidence. Use benchmarks, if possible.

STUDENT'S NAME: _____	
TUTOR'S NAME: _____	
A. Reading skill improvement	___/20%
B. Writing skill improvement	___/20%
C. Subject notebook quality	___/20%
D. Attendance	___/20%
E. Attitude	___/20%
Tutor's Tentative Mark	___/100%
F. Tutor's anecdotal comments:	
G. Teacher's anecdotal comments:	
Supervising teacher's awarded report card mark ___/100%	
(The student's final mark is determined by the teacher after reviewing supporting documentation during a teacher-tutor conference.)	

ANECDOTAL SUBSTANTIATION OF STUDENT'S TENTATIVE MARKS

To be submitted with student marks.

READING SKILL IMPROVEMENT

At first, J_____ certainly did not want to read, and if he did, would never try a word he did not know. He simply waited, hoping that I would give it to him. Because of this, he read in a slow, halting manner, with very little comprehension or enjoyment.

I used the "experience story" method with him every day for the first three weeks of tutoring, and he began to predict words rather than using just sounding out alone. Now, at the end of the term, he is relying more on predicting than sounding. His reading speed has improved a lot, and he likes most of the books he reads with me.

J_____'s reading vocabulary has really gone up. He has no trouble with comprehending the books we read most of the time, because I make sure I build his prior experience before we begin. However, he has some difficulty understanding many of the subject texts, which are not only too high for him but have many unfamiliar ideas he does not understand. I spoke with Mr. H_____, and he and I devised some alternative assignments for J_____. It looks like he is going to pass, even though he has great difficulty reading the books in Mr. H_____'s class.

Regardless, J_____'s reading assessments indicate that he is reading better by two years' growth (see attached reading assessments). From reading with him every day, I know that this is quite true, and both he and I are very excited about his progress.

20/20

WRITING SKILL IMPROVEMENT

Because J_____ now feels better about himself, he takes more care with his writing. It no longer looks so sloppy. While he is writing longer pieces, the sentences are often disjointed and sometimes the stories make little sense (see attached examples).

I think he still sees writing as a chore and certainly does not like the idea of second or third drafts yet. While he has made some progress in writing, it has not been very much as you can see. I hope he will show more progress next semester. I would like you to meet with the two of us to see if we can develop further strategies so that he will make the same rapid improvement in writing as he has in reading.

12/20

SUBJECT NOTEBOOK QUALITY

J_____'s notebook was helter-skelter at first and a lot of his notes were missing. I managed to get a list of main assignments from his subject teachers, and then we organized his binder. We go over them once a week, and now he is up to date in all areas.

15/20

ATTENDANCE

J_____'s attendance has been good, other than the week he was sick and the day's trip his science class took. In fact, his attendance has been far better for the tutor class than for other subjects. This may be because we get along so well and he knows I really like him. He did, however, miss two days for which he had no coverage. Still, he is certainly not the "skip artist" he used to be, and I think he deserves a high mark as a reward.

18/20

ATTITUDE

J_____'s attitude is very positive about everything except writing. He enjoys our sessions. With his sense of humour, he often gets us laughing, so I have a good time, too. He knows he has improved his reading, and I think that helps. He was very proud when I told him he had gone up over two years. Of course, I did not tell him his level in reading as you instructed.

15/20

OBSERVATIONS

J_____ does not work well when he is around R_____. I wonder if we could change rooms or alter our tutor time or something. I understand that the two of them act up in a number of different classes when they sit together, too. I wonder if all the subject teachers also realize this.

J_____ tells me he never has breakfast, and he has second lunch, which is really late in the day. No wonder he seems so tired sometimes. I have talked to him, but should I speak to Guidance or will you talk to him? Could we bring a snack up for him from the cafeteria during class as we work?

While J_____ does not read and write that well yet, I know he thinks and speaks well. In fact, he has taught me a lot, for he is really knowledgeable about a whole bunch of things. I think he is really going to improve next semester. Because we get along so well, I would like to be his tutor again next semester. I hope that can be arranged.

PS. My friend Angela C_____ really wants to be a tutor. She is thinking of becoming a teacher. Could she come and see you for an interview? I think she'll be terrific if she joins the class.

ELEMENTARY SCHOOL STUDENT'S PROFILE

This is to be used as a guide. Please write in anecdotal form without sub-headings. Use benchmarks, if possible.

Tutor's name: _____

Student's name: _____ **Sex:** ____ **Age:** ____ **Grade:** ____

Reading level: initial _____

current _____

SKILL PROGRESS: Please define growth in these areas by comparing your initial encounters with your student to your current relationship.

Reading: response to reading generally _____
ability to attend to meaning _____
ability to predict in context _____
vocabulary growth _____
ability to answer significant questions about content
strategies you introduced directly or indirectly and evidence that they were used. _____
Writing: response to writing generally _____
ability to communicate a story orally or graphically by generating meaning through drawing/printing or writing _____
quality and quantity of writing _____
where possible provide dated examples of samples or letter formation. _____
Social Skills: define improvements: use the social skills checklist in Chapter 7.

STUDENT ATTITUDE

compare initial attitude towards reading in general to current attitude _____ compare student's initial relationship with you and others (peers and adults) to current relationship _____
compare the ability of the student to focus his or her attention and respond to your directions and suggestions then and now _____ describe the ability of your student to stay on task then and now _____

TEACHING STRATEGIES

suggestions as to how the student might best be served in a one-to-one tutoring format _____
define techniques of teaching reading, writing and social skills that you have used or developed _____

SUMMARY

Write at length defining the progress your student has made in all areas through this one-to-one relationship with you.

Excerpts from Leading Authorities in Reading Theory Research

"Prediction is essential for reading; reading is in fact impossible without prediction.... Material from which the student is expected to learn to read must be potentially meaningful to him—otherwise there is no way he will be able to predict." *Smith*

"We regard comprehension as a direct function of prior knowledge....A reader must possess some background of experience that can be tied to the words he reads, or otherwise they can mean little indeed....Comprehension means relating new experiences to the already known." *Goodman*

"Print makes sense when readers can relate it to what they know already. It is therefore evident that both comprehension and learning depend on prior knowledge, or what the reader knows already." *Smith*

"If the teacher's intention is to improve reading, then students must have material they can easily understand. Teachers should strive to ensure that reading is easy and permit the children to judge whether materials or activities are too difficult, too incomprehensible, or too dull." *Rychman*

"Reading selections must be based on the students' interests, experiential background and reading level." *Miller*

"It appears that comprehension cannot be taught directly, but situations can be provided to facilitate and encourage the process of print into meaning." *Goodman*

"Comprehension is a state of achievement, thus it cannot be divided into subskills." *Pugh*

"Reading cannot be formally taught. Meaningless drills and exercise may teach children to score high on boring, repetitive and nonsensical tasks but such a specialized ability will not make readers of them." *Smith*

"Sequential skill instruction will interfere with comprehension since the learner's attention is diverted from meaning....The essential skills of reading cannot be taught, yet we have been teaching reading as a set of skills to be learned rather than as a language process to be mastered. What has saved us from even greater failure, considering how unsound our instructional programs have been, is the remarkable language learning ability of the children we teach." *Goodman*

"We must understand enough about the reading process and its acquisition to stop interfering with learners in the name of helping them." *Smith*

"Reading skills come primarily through the practice of reading; they are fostered rather than taught." *Rychman*

Examples Of Students' Writing Improvement

STUDENT A'S INITIAL WRITING

This student does not take pride in work, demonstrates shame, attempts to "blow it up" and obviously wants to write better than he does.

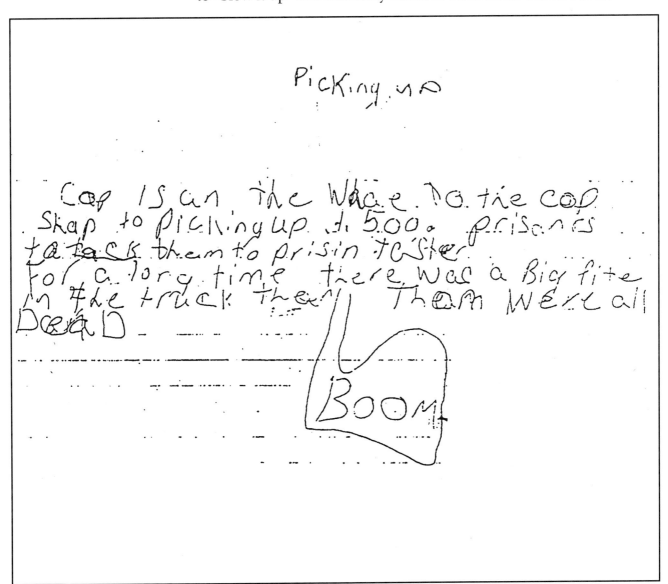

STUDENT A'S WRITING FIVE MONTHS LATER

Read creativity and pride in self. Notice the writing is copious. This is one of three pages. It has coherence, greater control and detail. It's not negative; it's imaginative and pure fun. He writes. This student became a volunteer Reading Tutor.

The Motorcycles

Richard and I were going out on our motorbikes to our friends house to ride around. We left about twelve o'clock. We rode around until we ran out of gas. We were in the woods and it was starting to get dark, so we decided to stay the night in the woods. We made a campfire. After we got the fire going, we dozed off to sleep.

The next thing I knew, a bunch of midgets on motorcycles showed up. There had to be at least twenty of them. Ten of them jumped me and ten of them jumped my friend and started to wrestle us. My friend and I thought they were kids, but they were a lot stronger than kids. All of a sudden this giant blue door opened underneath us. We fell through the door and so did our motorbikes.

When we woke up, there were things floating around! It looked like we had gone to the future. 5,000 years from now. When we looked at our bikes, they looked different. We filled them with gas. We started them up and when we went to move them. They weren't touching the ground. We were flying! We saw this big old house; it looked like something out of Dracula!

STUDENT B'S INITIAL WRITING

This student was labelled Learning Disabled and a lack of fine motor control was cited.

STUDENT B'S WRITING ONE YEAR LATER

This student moved to a higher level of endeavour and went on to college.

Picking Stones

Every spring and fall we pick stones. This year we had to pick 140 acres of stones. In the fall we use the tractor and loader and in the spring we use a tractor and trailer. This year we are building a stone bucket; it is 5 feet. It will go on the back of the tractor.

When picking stones it is harder you really sweat alot and get a gostan outside it took a couple weeks but we finally are done. Until we plow in the fall.

STUDENT C'S INITIAL WRITING

Labelled Educably Retarded.

Tafr:

I was DivAin (driving) dbawn the rode (rood) and
I saw a purse on the rode. I pet (put)
it up and I phonde (phoned) the ploces,
and I got a I1,0000 for a readwod (reword)
an I dote (bought) a dane new car it (It) was
a fans-a.m.
I would go to Jason an I pet (pick) he up
on way to calona (California) an we got a BMX. (truck)

STUDENT C'S WRITING FIVE MONTHS LATER

This student received his diploma on his own in grade twelve without a tutor's help.

48 Hours To Live

If I oney had 48 Hours to live, I would take 3 of my friends and 8 Girl. I would take ther to California and have fun and ~~~~ praty and buy a car ~~~~ amd ~~~~ speed ~~~~ boat and a ~~~~ house. and go to Disney land. and give my friend a $100.000.00 each and by a manchin for each of them. a coven ofor me and my friends and a larogrond. and lay a cataloc ~~~~ for ~~~~ my friend and send 500.000.00 ~~~~ to ethopen for they can have food and ~~~~ school and house for thay cod live in.

I would miss my friends my car. my speed loat my momey ~~~~ and California my famly and gril and live thi rest of my

STUDENT D'S INITIAL WRITING

Classified as aggressive.

I stold "20.00 in the parse and the drove the car and The cop folled Me I stost shoot the Kopp and stold th e c pee curc. I bleoow the car and drove a way im the twrck and kill a man and rodder a sore

STUDENT D'S WRITING ONE YEAR LATER

Now somewhat less aggressive. Concerned about social issues. Proud of his cursive writing.

Sample of Examination Marks

Below is a partial list of the final examination marks of students deemed Exceptional who had reading tutors. All of these students were socially promoted and had never passed an examination before. Such results have the reciprocal effect of further motivating the student to do well.

STUDENT		SUBJECT	MARK
A	NFC 2B2	74%	(Highest mark in class)
B	SNC 2B2	84%	
C	SNC 2B0	72%	
D	GCA 1B0/1B2	60%	
E	PHF 1B2	74%	(Highest mark in class)
F	SNC 3B2	74%	
G	HCA 2B2	76%	(Highest mark in class)
H	SNC 1B2	87%	(Highest mark in class)
I	SNC 1B2	81%	
J	BKA 2B2	99%	(Highest mark in class)

Enjoyment in learning is a crucial element of success in school.

Accommodation An adaptive process that results in the altering of perceptions.

Absolute Standard A standard for all that does not make allowances for individual differences among students-not used in this program.

Analogy A resemblance between things otherwise unlike.

Assimilation The taking in of new ideas or concepts into already existing categories of perception.

Behaviour Modification In this text, positive reinforcement for desirable behaviour.

Benchmarks Standards of student achievement which are samples of student performance on a wide range of language and mathematics tasks, providing insight into student performance and achievement.

Cognition The intellectual process of knowing.

Consonant A sound in speech other than a vowel expressed by a letter or letters.

Cueing System The systems of syntax and semantics that act in concert with one's experiential base to facilitate prediction in reading.

English as a Second Language (ESL) A term used to describe learning English as a second or additional language. English is not the mother tongue.

English Skills Development (ESD) A course designed to meet the needs of those students who are new to the country and whose educational background has gaps that must be closed so they may reach their full potential within the school system. Used when describing a student who does not have literacy skills in his or her first language.

Experiential Base An individual's world knowledge—all that one knows.

Fossilization The systematic and continuous use of erroneous semantic or syntactic forms.

Functional Reading Level A level of reading ability that gives an individual the opportunity to cope effectively with the general day to day world of reading.

Exceptional Students Those students deemed quite different from the norm.

Learning Outcomes The products of student's individual work.

Letters The graphic symbols (the print) on paper that stand for words and meanings.

Linguistics The study of language, in particular its sounds, meanings and syntax.

Mentoring A big brother/big sister function.

Metaphor An expression of one thing in terms of another: "My love is a red, red rose."

Miscue	A miscue is a word uttered by a reader which is not the exact word printed on the page. It may be either positive (fits meaning) or negative (distorts meaning).
Phoneme	The smallest unit of speech sound that distinguishes one utterance from another.
Phonics	A reading strategy that depends on the translation of a letter symbol into its sound with or without comprehension.
Prediction	The strongest reading strategy. It's prompted only by the act of comprehension of a passage gained through access to prior knowledge.
Prior Knowledge	The information one has about a reading topic prior to reading the passage.
Psycholinguistics	A field of psychology that investigates how people learn and use language. (A development of insights into how the brain processes information of a graphic nature.)

Reading Levels:

Independent	The reading level at which an individual can read and comprehend fully without any assistance from a teacher, or tutor.
Instructional	The reading level at which an individual requires a teacher's assistance with vocabulary and comprehension. This is the potential growth level of reading.
Frustrational	The reading level at which an individual cannot acquire meaning from print. The only outcome of a student reading at this level is a greater distaste for reading. This level is two years or more above a person's instructional level.

Semantics	The word knowledge in a language essential to prediction and, consequently, comprehension in reading.
Standards	Standards of student achievement which are samples of student performance on a wide range of language and mathematics tasks, providing insight into student performance and achievement.

Structures:

Surface	The printed information on a page that must be interpreted by a reader.
Deep	Word knowledge, or the meanings of words and concepts (both denotations and connotations) that allow the reader access to the comprehension of surface structures.

Syntax	The word order in language essential to word prediction in context.
Transfer of Learning	The use of one's experiences and concepts to interpret and comprehend new, yet similar concepts—the application of knowledge to new situations.